PACES
PACES
PACES
PACES

Jo M. Stanchfield

Harvey R. Granite

CONSULTANT: Millard H. Black

BOARD OF EDUCATION

 Houghton Mifflin Company • BOSTON

Atlanta • Dallas • Geneva, Illinois • Hopewell, New Jersey • Palo Alto • Toronto

VISTAS
A READING ACHIEVEMENT PROGRAM

HORIZONS

SUMMITS

TEMPOS

PACES

NETWORKS

PATTERNS

Library of Congress Catalog Card Number: 77-83336

ISBN: 0-395-25228-8

ACKNOWLEDGMENTS

For each of the selections listed below, grateful acknowledgment is made for permission to adapt and/or reprint original material, as follows:

"Augusta Savage," from *Six Black Masters of American Art,* by Romare Bearden and Harry Henderson. Copyright © 1972 by Romare Bearden and Harry Henderson. Reprinted by permission of Doubleday & Company, Inc.

"Bermuda Triangle," from "The Mystery of the Bermuda Triangle," by Charles Berlitz, published in the *Children's Digest.* Copyright © 1975 by Charles Berlitz. Reprinted by permission of Doubleday & Co., Inc.

"Bicycle Styles: Yesterday and Today," an edited excerpt from *Bikes,* by Stephen C. Henkel. Copyright © 1972 by Stephen C. Henkel. All rights reserved. Reprinted by permission of The Chatham Press, Old Greenwich, Conn.

"The Blue Bike," from "The Girl with the Fifteen Speeds," by John Savage. Copyright © 1967 by Downe Publishing, Inc. Reprinted by permission of Curtis Brown, Ltd.

"Blue Winds Dancing," by Thomas S. Whitecloud. Reprinted by permission of Mrs. Barbara Whitecloud.

"The Bread-Crumb Tango," by E. M. Hunnicutt. Reprinted by permission of the author and *Boys' Life,* published by the Boy Scouts of America.

"The Case of the Punjabi Ruby," by Frank Willment. Reprinted by permission from *Plays, The Drama Magazine for Young People.* Copyright © 1976 by Plays, Inc. This play is for reading purposes only. For permission to produce this play, write to Plays, Inc., 8 Arlington St., Boston, Ma. 02116.

"Cheryl Toussaint, Somebody Special," from *Women Who Win,* by Francene Sabin. Copyright © 1975 by Francene Sabin. Adapted by permission of Random House, Inc.

"Diaries Are for Secrets," by Ruth E. Hampton. Adapted from *Young World* magazine. Copyright © 1976 by The Saturday Evening Post Company, Indianapolis, Indiana. Used by permission.

"Diary of the Hauter Experiment," from *Notes on the Hauter Experiment,* by Bernice Grohskopf. Used by permission of Atheneum Publishers.

"The Eskimo Widow," from *The Firebringer and Other Great Stories,* by Louis Untermeyer. Copyright © 1968 by Louis Untermeyer. Reprinted by permission of the publishers, M. Evans & Company, Inc., New York, N.Y. 10017.

"Faces," from *Collected Poems,* by Sara Teasdale. Copyright 1920 by Macmillan Publishing Co., Inc. Renewed 1948 by Mamie T. Wheless. Reprinted with permission of Macmillan Publishing Co., Inc.

"Famous Black Americans," adapted from *Quiz Book on Black America,* by Clarence N. Blake and Donald F. Martin. Copyright © 1976 by Clarence N. Blake. Copyright © 1976 by Donald F. Martin. Reprinted by permission of Houghton Mifflin Company.

"Fetch!" by Robb White. Reprinted by permission of the author and *Boys' Life,* published by the Boy Scouts of America.

"Fifteen Honest Coins," from *Chinese*

CONTENTS

Naantam's Last Visit

by Mary Joyce Capps

Yellow Leaf, separated from her family at the age of three, was found and raised by Cagle, a trapper. Then very suddenly, Cagle died, leaving fifteen-year-old Yellow Leaf to take care of herself.

The summer raced away almost before she noticed. With the first heavy frosts, Yellow Leaf competed with the gray squirrels for nuts that fell. She burst into laughter as a squirrel darted up a tree and chattered its outrage at her. "There are enough nuts for both of us," she scolded. But the squirrel twitched its tail and scampered into a hole in the hollow tree. From there, it watched as she filled her basket.

1

All but one of Yellow Leaf's needs were taken care of. She had a snug home, food, and enough fuel to last the winter. She had freed Cagle's horse, so it could find food for itself. She hoped to find the horse again in the spring. But her desire for companionship could not be satisfied. It was a constant hunger that food and drink could not lessen. With Cagle now gone, Yellow Leaf yearned to be with her own people.

Two days after the first blizzard, Yellow Leaf returned from running the line of traps near the lake. She was clumsy and bearlike in the heavy furs she wore to protect herself from the bitter cold. Kneeling, she groaned with fatigue as she slipped the bundle of frozen game off her back and turned to stir up the fire. The traps had been hard to find under the fresh snow, and her catch had been small — only two rabbits and a young wolf.

Later, as Yellow Leaf knelt before the fire, cooking bits of meat over the flames, she was startled by a soft cry from the pile of game that was thawing near the fire.

She poked the pile with a stick and leaped back as the wolf stirred feebly and stared up at her. He bared his sharp teeth, and growls rumbled from deep in his throat. The Indian girl crouched, then raised the stick and crept closer to aim a crushing blow at the animal's head.

As she stood over the helpless wolf, Yellow Leaf was suddenly shaken by the brave helplessness in the stricken animal's eyes. For a few seconds, the two stared into each other's faces — a look that sparked, for a moment, a bond of kinship in the girl. Cagle had never allowed her to have a pet. Animals were for food and fur, nothing more. Yellow Leaf was confused by the rush of pity she felt. The wolf's coat was beautiful. It would have been her first good pelt.

Yellow Leaf turned and put some of the meat she had been cooking on the end of the stick. She offered him the meat gingerly. As the starved wolf tried to draw back, his growls rose, then changed to sad whimpers as his useless hind legs refused to move. The trap had hurt his back.

Again the girl offered the food. The wild one drooled in

hunger, but he would not eat. Yellow Leaf removed the meat from the stick and tossed it near him.

The Indian girl toasted more meat over the fire and ate it, watching the animal as he stretched his nose closer to the food. Whining, he sniffed it, turning his yellowish-brown eyes to stare at the girl, who watched without moving. The animal had seen few humans, but his every instinct warned him of danger. Yellow Leaf watched as the wolf twisted and turned, straining to straighten his legs. Again she felt the sudden rush of sympathy and understanding as the wolf turned his yearning eyes toward the door. He laid his long head on his forepaws and bravely prepared to die.

When Yellow Leaf awoke at dawn, she was surprised to find the wolf still living. He growled threateningly, then fiercely bared his fangs as Yellow Leaf sat up. She quickly reached for the heavy stick, then laid it aside when she saw that he was still helpless and had not moved.

Suddenly she laughed. The wolf had lapped the water from a pot she had shoved near him, and the chunk of meat had been eaten. Somehow, though they were enemies, it gave her a warm feeling to have a living creature to share her home and food. It eased her feeling of loneliness to know that eyes were watching as she moved about the cabin. "I shall call you Naantam, which means 'wolf,' " she said.

Naantam's injured back was healing slowly, and he limped around the cabin now. But Yellow Leaf was still frightened of the wolf, even though she knew she would never be able to kill him. So one day, Yellow Leaf offered Naantam his freedom by leaving the door open. Tears began to roll down her cheeks as the animal quickly rose and crossed the cabin to leave her. For about a minute, the wolf stood in the doorway, ears perked, hungrily sniffing the frigid air. His body trembled with eagerness. Then his ears twitched at the sound of a low sob, and the yellowish-brown eyes looked back at Yellow Leaf. More tears, but of happiness now, slipped down her face when

Naantam unexpectedly returned and curled up in front of the fire. The animal didn't want to leave her! Did Naantam feel affection for her, or did he merely sense that he was still too weak to survive in such bitter weather? One icy morning, she awoke to find Naantam curled on the bed fur at the bottom of her bunk. Now she was no longer afraid of Naantam.

Day after day, Yellow Leaf tended her traps with Naantam limping along beside her. The wolf made no attempt to hunt or escape. He seemed content with the rabbits and other small game the girl shared with him. Her pile of pelts seemed disappointingly small, compared to Cagle's, despite all her hard work. But the cold was gradually tapering off. It would soon be spring. Naantam seemed to sense it too. He had begun to leave her now, and sometimes she did not see him for several days. She was lonely without Naantam, but she knew he would have to return to the forest for good when she began her trip west, for she wanted to find some of her people. She hoped Naantam would not have too much to relearn in the wilds. Cagle had been wise not to let her tame wild things, she decided. It handicapped them, and how could they tell which humans to trust and which to avoid?

When Naantam stayed away for two weeks, Yellow Leaf decided he would not return again. She prayed that the animal had not been killed but perhaps had found a mate or joined a pack, which was as it should be. The frozen lake had water showing now, far out from the bank. The dawn and evening skies were often patched with bright blue against the stormy gray. Winter was dying. She would be preparing to leave soon.

Lost in her thoughts as she returned to the cabin from the traps, she felt torn about leaving. She stepped out of the trees and into the clearing in front of the cabin. Fright clutched at her throat when she saw five Indian men. Their leader had dismounted from Cagle's horse! They were between her and the cabin. It was impossible to run in the clumsy snowshoes. She was trapped!

Rudely the men demanded food. Yellow Leaf nodded, trying to conceal her fear.

"Where is your man?" the leader demanded, pointing to the two sets of snowshoe tracks in the snow.

Hope and relief flooded over the frightened girl. She had used Cagle's larger snowshoes for two days before repairing her own. The men had noticed the different sizes and thought a husband or father was also living in the cabin.

She pointed back toward the lake. "He is tending his traps and will return soon," she replied steadily. Her heart was pounding. She hoped the lie would make them go away.

All of a sudden, menacing growls sounded from behind her, and fear showed on the faces of the Indians. After being gone so long, Naantam had appeared from nowhere. The wolf was crouched on the snowy slope slightly behind her, fangs bared and eyes gleaming! He was obviously protecting her.

The men grouped closer together, then fell back in confusion as she walked to the huge wolf, put her hand on the raised ridge of fur down his back, and talked soothingly to Naantam.

"I will hold the wolf while you leave," Yellow Leaf told them calmly. "And that is my man's horse you have found. Thank you for returning it."

For a heart-stopping moment, Yellow Leaf was afraid she had gone too far in demanding the return of Cagle's horse. The leader stiffened, and anger flashed in his black eyes. He looked from her to the wolf, standing quietly now but with watchful, restless eyes scanning the group.

Yellow Leaf withdrew her hand from Naantam's back. The wolf immediately crouched again, showing powerful muscles that were ready to attack. His huge upper jaw wrinkled as he showed his teeth. "Naantam will spring if you make any move toward us," she warned as the leader signaled one of his men, whose fingers inched toward a knife at his belt. The creeping fingers hesitated, then stopped.

Spots of angry red burned on the leader's cheeks, and he still held firmly to the rope around the horse's neck. It was an impasse. Yellow Leaf realized she had disgraced

him. She would have to offer him an honorable way out of the deadlock.

"I am sorry I cannot prepare food for you," Yellow Leaf said. "I am ashamed of Naantam's bad manners, but you can see that he does not like strangers. I don't dare remove my hands to cook. But I have just taken three fat rabbits. I would be happy if you will accept them as a gift for returning our horse. I can throw them to one of your men, then hold the wolf until you have gone."

The leader considered her offer, then nodded and dropped the horse's rope. When the girl again placed her hand on the wolf's head, the leader turned and walked into the woods. He walked with new dignity. He did not look back as the nearest Indian caught the bundle of rabbits Yellow Leaf threw. He and the remaining men faded silently into the forest.

Trembling and stiff from her tense position in the cold, Yellow Leaf sagged down in the snow. She placed her arms around Naantam's neck and buried her face in his silvery-tipped brown fur. The men would not return.

Naantam had come back for what proved to be his last visit, and he had repaid Yellow Leaf for sparing his life.

Showdown on the Tundra

The day it happened, I had decided to take a walk after work on the night shift. Work was on the north slope of the Brooks Range in Alaska. It was May 1974. I had taken a job on the trans-Alaska pipeline at one of the camps in the mountains.

To the south, the mountains looked like upside-down *V*'s —steep and foreboding. To the north were the rolling hills that sloped down to the Arctic Ocean, one hundred miles away. I decided to walk north with my camera, so I could get a picture of the camp with the rugged mountains as a background.

It was four in the morning when I set off. There was enough light for a good picture as the arctic summer was upon us. I had been walking for fifteen minutes when I came across an antler, three feet long, bleached white by the sun, that a caribou had shed. It would make a perfect addition to the picture. I could lay it on a small hill and frame the camp inside the curved antler. It had six sharp tines on it, two of which were broken. Carrying the antler, I walked for another hour toward the hill from which I had decided to take the picture.

"Showdown on the Tundra" is adapted from the *Reader's Digest* condensation of the story by Ron Rau that originally appeared in the May 12, 1975 issue of SPORTS ILLUSTRATED. © 1975 Time Inc.

Then I saw the wolf, just fifty yards away. It was coming into my path at an angle, in that unusual bouncing walk wolves and coyotes have. I stopped. The wolf kept walking until it was directly in front of me. Then it turned and looked at me as though it had known all along I was there.

My first response was to look for other wolves. The tundra was treeless and rolling, with many gullies and small hills. This is why I had not seen it earlier. It had just come out of a ditch. There it stood, on those very long legs, staring at me. The nearest tree was at least a hundred miles away, but still I thought about it. All I had with which to protect myself were the caribou antler and a jackknife.

"Wolves seldom, if ever, attack," I said to myself. But there stood the animal fifty yards away, with the hairs on the back of its neck raised — an animal that could kill me. Did it know that?

I knew that I could not show fear. If the wolf sensed that I was afraid . . . well, I could be in trouble. Maybe I was already.

I can't say how long we looked at each other — ten seconds, thirty, a minute maybe. I thought hard, fast. There was no place to run, no place to hide. I was two miles from camp. The only thing I could do was to take the offensive and show the wolf that I was not a person to be fooled with.

I decided to take my chances with the caribou antler. It was heavy enough and stout, and the tines were six to eight inches long. If it came to a showdown, I would go for its ribs, hoping that a tine would go in between two of them into the lungs. I would have my jackknife opened in my left hand.

Then the wolf began to circle.

I forgot about the knife.

I began walking toward camp, directly in line with the wolf. It stopped. I stopped. I noticed I was downwind from it. Perhaps when it smelled me, it would be scared away. After all, I was a human. "Hadn't we ruled the earth for thousands and thousands of years? Yes," I thought, "but not with a caribou antler. Even primitive people

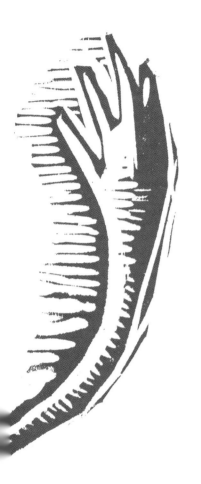

would have been better armed — they would at least have had a spear."

The wolf started circling again. I started walking. It stopped. We studied each other. The wolf was grayish-yellow and weighed about eighty pounds — half my weight. And still it could kill me. But what a grand creature — those long, powerful, slender, fast-moving legs so perfectly designed for the tundra.

I began walking again, and so did the wolf. I forced my mind back to the caribou antler, which was my real security. "Go for the ribs. The antler will probably break if you hit the wolf on the skull," I told myself. I kept looking at the tines. If only I had time to sharpen them on a rock. Then I would have something. They were about as sharp as a table knife.

The wolf stopped. I stopped. Then it sat down facing me. I longed to know what was going on in its mind. It surely wasn't afraid, for people were new to this land. It was too far from the ocean for the Eskimos to bother with and too far north for the Athapascan Indians.

I decided to make the next move — toward camp. The wolf was sitting on my left, far off the line to camp, but still only fifty yards away. It had been circling carefully, getting neither closer nor farther away. I took a step, and the wolf leaped to its feet as though stung by a bee. I stopped, frozen in midstep. It circled, and I began walking again. Then it stopped, facing me, and I could clearly see its raised neck hairs. I growled, a well-thought-out growl. Again I studied the caribou antler. It was a little long for a quick swing, a little heavy for close hand-to-hand combat — no — hand-to-teeth combat. Go for the ribs.

Then it moved — this time directly at me.

I moved toward the wolf, growling. We moved a dozen steps toward each other before we both stopped. Five seconds passed. I knew what I had to do. I had to make the next move.

I stepped toward the wolf, and it leaped six feet to one side as though stung again. Then it retreated those dozen steps it had taken earlier — back to its fifty-yard distance.

My whole body swelled with relief. It had retreated. It had shown fear or at least the next-best thing to fear — confusion. For the first time, I realized that I was shaking. But it was over, wasn't it? The wolf *had* retreated.

I turned away and began walking toward camp. The wolf was off to the side, circling again, wanting to get downwind for a smell. I speeded up.

"Don't walk too fast!" I shouted inside my mind. It might sense fear. So I stopped and faced the wolf again. We were now seventy-five yards apart, too far for me to see if the hairs on its neck were still raised. We stared at each other; then I turned and began walking again.

This time I did not stop. If the wolf followed, I knew what I would do. I should have done it in the first place. I would stop and lash my jackknife to the end of the antler. I could use a bootlace. "Perhaps I should stop and do it now," I thought. "No, keep walking." The wolf was following my trail, sniffing my tracks and raising its nose to the wind. I went into a gully. The wolf was out of sight.

Five minutes passed, and I had not seen it. I walked rapidly, straight for the camp. Fifteen minutes passed — no wolf. For the first time I felt safe — no, overjoyed. I found that I had developed a very warm feeling for my caribou antler. Without it, I might have acted differently. I might not have had the nerve to walk at the wolf with only a jackknife. I wondered what the wolf had in mind when it came at me. What would have happened if I had panicked and run? What would I have done without the antler?

Soon I was standing on a small hill three hundred yards from camp. I could smell bacon. The day shift had just gotten up and was going to breakfast. The sun had cleared the mountain to the east. It was a beautiful morning.

I stood on the rise, wondering what to do with the antler. I could take it with me on the plane when I left, but it would cheapen the value of the antler to take it away. It had served me well. I would always have it anyway, in my mind.

I dropped it to the ground. Like a fake Hollywood chair, it broke in half.

THE ESKIMO WIDOW

by Louis Untermeyer

In the coldest part of the Arctic Zone, the Eskimos have a legend they tell when the long winter nights are at their worst. The story is about a little old woman who lived in the northernmost part of Alaska and who lived alone. Unable to do her own hunting or fishing, she lived on what her neighbors gave her. It was a poor village. The neighbors had little to spare. So most of the time, she was as hungry as she was lonely.

One morning, she heard a noise that sounded like a child crying. When she could no longer ignore it, she went outside and found a bundle of matted fur on the ice. It was a baby polar bear whose mother had been caught and who had managed to crawl away before the hunters could kill him. The helplessness of the cub moved the old woman's lonely heart. Without thinking how she might care for him, she carried him in and gave him some scraps that she had been saving for her next meal. He ate them eagerly, yawned, and fell asleep.

Now she was no longer alone. She cared for the cub as though he were her child. She gave him half of what little food she got. As a result, she was hungrier than ever. But she was happy. Once in a while, when the Eskimos made a great catch, everyone in the village was given part of it, and the old woman and her cub would feast for a few days. Most of the time, though, everyone went hungry.

Somehow, the old woman survived, and somehow, the cub got fat. Then he grew lean and tall. One day, after he had become the most important thing in her life, he disappeared. That night the old woman could not sleep. "My child! My child!" she moaned. The next morning, she cried again, but this time it was a cry of joy. Her cub had returned with a fine catch of salmon. He had taught himself how to fish.

As he grew up, he became a clever hunter. No longer a cub, the young bear caught not only fish but, once in a while, small seals. There was plenty now for both of them. Soon there was enough to share with the neighbors. Everyone remarked what a smart bear he was. "My child," she repeated proudly.

But the good days did not last long. Suddenly the weather changed. For weeks, blinding snowstorms swept over the village. Not a fish could be caught. The seals seemed to have swum away.

It was then that one of the villagers had a plan. "Why should we starve," he said, "when we have food right here? The old woman's bear has plenty of flesh beneath that fur. He should make good eating."

The others said nothing, but they plowed through shoulder-high snowdrifts to the old woman's house. There they found the widow weeping. The bear had disappeared again.

The villagers slowly walked back to their homes. There was nothing to say, nothing to do. The storms grew worse. There seemed to be no hope for the starving village.

Then one day the wind changed, and the bear came back. Everyone stared at him. No one spoke. The widow, a little bundle of bones, was too weak to call out, but she managed a cracked smile. The bear did not stir from where he stood. But he lifted his head again and again.

"He's trying to tell us something," said a villager. "I think he wants us to go with him," said one of the others. "He seems to be pointing."

The bear started to walk away. The villagers followed him. He led them over hills of ice, skirting wide deep cracks. Finally he stopped. A hundred yards in front of him, there was a dark mass barely moving on a large piece of ice. As the villagers went closer, they saw it was a wounded but still ferocious animal, a huge bull seal. The seal was larger than any one of them had ever caught. Here was food to last a long, long time — plenty of meat and an endless supply of blubber, the fat that would put new life into the people of the whole village.

It was a happy group that brought back the food and the bear. Both were welcomed, especially the bear.

"He knew what we needed," the people told each other, "and he found it for us."

"He didn't just find it," said one of the villagers. "He fought it for us. We owe everything to him."

"We owe everything to him," the people repeated. "And we will never forget him."

The widow waited until the bear walked over and put his head in her hand. Then she patted the furry head. "My child," she said softly.

Morning Mood

I wake with morning yawning in my mouth,
With laughter, see a teakettle spout steaming.
I wake with hunger in my belly
And I lie still, so beautiful it is, it leaves me dazed,
The timelessness of the light.

Grandma cares for me, and our family needs nothing more.
They share each other for pleasure
As mother knows, who learns of happiness
From her own actions
They did not even try to be beautiful, only true,
But beauty is here, it is a custom.

This place of unbroken joy,
Giving out its light today — only today — not tomorrow.

                    M. Panegoosho

The Bread-Crumb Tango

by E. M. Hunnicutt

Nobody was too surprised when Harley got the best part in the school play. That's not saying everyone was happy about it. Harley is a good actor. You have to say that for him. But he always wants to change a play around to make his own part bigger. Creativity is what he calls it.

Take the play we did last spring. Two days before we put on the play, Harley talked Mr. Bradley, our drama coach, into letting him rewrite the second act. On opening night, Harley was great. But the rest of us had trouble remembering all our new lines.

Then once there was a big scene that didn't have Harley in it. He worked his dog into the story in some way. The dog barked so much it drowned out everybody. Harley was the star that night, too — the only actor the audience could hear unless you count the dog.

When the list of people in the play went up on the bulletin board, I saw I had the second-best part. "Harley," I said to him, "the play is the thing. It's more important than the part of any one person."

"Of course the play is the thing, John," he said with that frown he gets when he is thinking. "That's why we want to make the play as good as we possibly can."

"It's already good," I said. "Why don't we leave it alone?"

But instead of answering me, he started making notes on his clipboard. That clipboard is supposed to make him look like a Broadway director.

The play was a fairy tale, *Hansel and Gretel.* We were going to put it on for small children on a Saturday afternoon. Harley was the witch. It was really a girl's part, but he'll do anything to get on the stage. He has this big idea about becoming a famous actor someday. I was Hansel, the one who pushes the witch into the oven. I was kind of looking forward to it. Kathy Marcus was Gretel.

Harley's clipboard was full of notes by the first rehearsal. "The witch shouldn't die," he said in a loud voice. "She should tell Hansel and Gretel she's sorry for what she has done. Then, with a happy heart, she should sing this little song I've written."

Mr. Bradley said no to that one.

One of the theater classes started building the set. Harley thought his oven should be bigger.

"Harley," Kathy said, "not bigger but hotter. Or you'll come out half-baked."

But it was no joke to Harley. He started writing himself into the first act. While Hansel and Gretel are going through the woods, dropping their bread crumbs, he wanted to have the witch in the background doing a modern dance. He called it the *Bread-Crumb Tango.*

Mr. Bradley said no to that idea too. I think he was still

a little upset about Harley's dog. He told Harley to stick to the script.

"But Harley won't," Kathy said to me one day after rehearsal. "When he gets in front of that audience, he'll pull something. If everything else fails, he can always rattle the door of his oven."

"At least the audience will only be little kids," I said.

"Let's see some respect for little kids!" she shot back. "Without them I'd be really poor."

Kathy baby-sits a lot.

Then one day, Uncle Fred flew into town. He was stopping here on one of his trips from the West Coast. Uncle Fred is my all-time-favorite relative. He used to play pro football. When he arrived, he had tickets for the football game on Saturday. He always does. Uncle Fred sees more football games than some coaches.

"I can't go with you," I had to tell him. "I have to be in this play."

So, of course, he decided to come to the play. "You won't like it," I said. "It's little-kid stuff."

He said *Hansel and Gretel* was a big favorite of his. So Uncle Fred gave the tickets for the game to my parents.

The audience on Saturday looked like the people in *Gulliver's Travels*. There was a giant uncle Fred sitting out there surrounded by little people.

"Who's that man?" Kathy asked, peeping out through the curtain.

"That's my uncle Fred. Look, don't let Harley know there's anyone special out there. He'll ham it up just that much more."

"I don't know why he's so silly."

"I guess Harley doesn't think he's silly," I said without thinking about it. Then I thought about it. Harley's big idea of becoming a famous actor was serious to *him*. "Kathy," I said, "I think someone *really* important in the audience would scare him to death."

So I walked over to Harley, putting it all together in my head as I went — the way he does. Maybe I'd been around Harley too long because the story that came out was almost *pure* creativity.

"Harley," I said, "there's a talent scout out front." I wondered if he would believe such a wild story.

But I didn't have to worry. Harley took a quick peek through the curtain and saw Uncle Fred. "Is he from the Civic Theater?" Harley had been living in his make-believe world for so long that he would believe anything.

"Let's say he's from something larger," I said.

"The university?"

"I won't say any more. I wouldn't want to make you nervous just before putting on a play. Let's just say he is known nationwide."

Harley turned a little pale and began tugging at his witch costume. Then I put the icing on the cake. "He's flying back to New York tonight."

Kathy came up to me a minute later. "It's beautiful," she said. "Harley is just standing over there whispering, 'Broadway, Broadway.' Except —"

"Except what?"

"I wish you could have done it without telling such a big lie."

"Lie!" I grinned. I put on the little hat that makes Hansel look seven years old. "Let's see some respect for a nice little kid like me!"

Harley did a good job acting even if he was scared. But sometimes his voice was almost too soft to be heard. When the time came for me to push him into the oven, he gave a funny little hop and a skip and jumped in himself. "Nice footwork, Harley," I whispered. "A real *Bread-Crumb Tango!*"

When we went out to take our bow, Kathy whispered to me, "When this is over, quickly slip out the back. When Harley finds out the truth, he won't let you out of here alive."

Uncle Fred clapped so much we had to go back for a second bow. "My uncle *is* a talent scout," I whispered to Kathy as the curtain came down. "I told the truth. He scouts for the New York Jets."

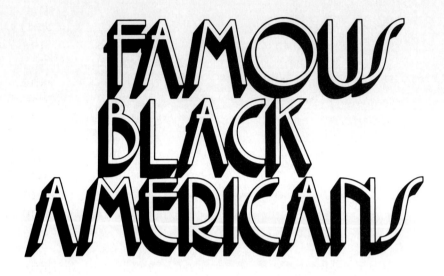

FAMOUS BLACK AMERICANS

by Clarence N. Blake and Donald F. Martin

How well do you know these famous people? See if you can match each of the following names with one of the paragraphs that follow. Then check your answers with the ones given upside-down on page 25.

Duke Ellington   Jesse Owens
Harriet Tubman   Diana Ross
Flip Wilson   Althea Gibson

1. She became one of the most outstanding black women tennis players of all time. She was born in Silver, South Carolina, in 1927, and was brought up in Harlem, New York. This great player was the first black woman to win the women's United States national singles title and the British national singles title at Wimbledon.

Adapted from *Quiz Book on Black America,* by Clarence N. Blake and Donald F. Martin.

2. She failed to win a part in her high-school musical play. Then she signed up for a singing class at school and quit because she was afraid that she would not do well. Her childhood home was a third-floor walkup in Detroit. Singing was always a part of her life. On Sundays, she sang hymns with the congregation at the Baptist Church and then later as a member of the choir. She became part of a singing group called the Primettes. The Primettes later became the Supremes, and she was on her way to becoming a millionaire.

3. Born in 1899, he was a band leader, pianist, and a jazz composer of national and international fame. He was seventeen years old when he wrote his first piece of music, "Soda Fountain Rag." In 1969, he was given the Presidential Medal of Freedom.

4. She was an abolitionist, born in Dorchester County, Maryland. Born into slavery, she worked as a field hand until 1859, when she escaped to the North. She decided that her life's work would be to lead other slaves to freedom through the Underground Railroad. To this end, she helped more than three hundred slaves gain freedom. Between trips, she worked as a cook and spoke at Boston anti-slavery meetings. During the Civil War, she worked with the Union troops as a nurse and as a spy behind Confederate lines. After the war, she kept working for her people, setting up a home for needy blacks in Auburn, New York.

5. Born in Alabama, he is an American track-and-field star. Believed to be the greatest track athlete of the century, he first showed his outstanding skill while in high school in Cleveland, Ohio. In 1935, as a member of the Ohio State University track team, he broke three world records and tied a fourth in one day. At the Olympic games in 1936, he won four gold medals by equaling the world record in the 100-meter race (10.3 seconds), by breaking the world record in the 200-meter race (20.7 seconds) and also in the broad jump

(26 feet, 5 5/16 inches), and by being the last member in the winning 400-meter relay.

6. He began the race for success in show business at the age of nine, when he was given a small part in a school play about the famous nurse Clara Barton. At the last minute, the girl who was supposed to play Clara got sick, and he was the only one who knew all the lines. So he got the part. He recalls, "I didn't decide right then and there to go into show business. I enjoyed making other kids laugh, and it was also rather easy for me. But show business was not on my mind. I used my natural voice for Clara Barton. I didn't try to sound like a girl. Just having that many lines was exciting enough for me because, until then, I was just going to be a wounded soldier in the play with nothing to do but groan."

---

1. Althea Gibson 2. Diana Ross 3. Duke Ellington 4. Harriet Tubman 5. Jesse Owens 6. Flip Wilson

Survival Skill

Reading Entertainment Schedules

TV Guide

On Thursday evening, Stella decided to stay home and watch a television show. She wasn't sure which shows were on that evening, so she checked the newspaper. Most newspapers print a daily guide to TV shows. The guide lists the times, the channels, the names and kinds of shows, and sometimes descriptions of the shows.

Look at the part of a TV guide that is on the next page. It gives the shows that are on television between 6:00 and 9:30 P.M. Which channels are listed? They are 2, 4, 5, 6, 7, 10, 11, 48, and 61. At 6:00, 7:00, 7:30, 8:30, and 9:00 P.M., channels 6 and 11 are listed together beside the same show. What does this mean? Yes, at those times, the same program is shown on both channels. Both are CBS stations. But you probably can get one channel more clearly than the other.

Now read the name of the 8:00 P.M. show on channel 2. What kind of movie is *The Right Hand*? It is a drama. What does "(1976)" mean after "Drama"? This movie was made in 1976. After the title of the movie, a short description of the plot is given. From this description, you can decide if you would be interested in seeing this movie. Are the major actors listed? Yes, Sue Spiegel and Jordan Miller are listed after the description. How long is this movie? That's right, it will last for two and a half hours. How do you know that? The length of time is given in parentheses after the names of the actors. Let's say that you want to go to bed at 10:00 P.M. You probably would not want to see this movie because you would not be able to see the end of it.

Now look at the show on channel 7 at 6:00 P.M. How long is this game? Although the length of time is not given, you know that it lasts for half an hour because at 6:30, another show is listed for channel 7.

Read the listing for channel 5 at 7:00. Has this show been on television before? Yes, "(Repeat)" means that "Sundown" has already been shown this year.

EVENING

6:00

(2) News—Baines, Schultz

(4) News—Shingai, McLane

(5) News—Farmer, Polk

(6) (11) News—Rico Lopez

(7) Strike It Rich—Game

(10) Villa Alegre—Education

(48) Strike Ten—Game

(61) Movie—Western (1954)
A Summer to Remember. Sheriff Earl Hunter brings law and order to a small frontier town. Al Garber. (2½ hrs.)

6:30

(2) Sports Recall—Discussion

(7) News—Cindy Phillips

(10) Ana Del Aire—Serial

(48) Guess Again—Game

7:00

(2) ABC News

(4) NBC News

(5) Sundown—Science Fiction
Mysterious events occur on the Kingston's Starship. Ron Kohl, Sarah Lee. (Repeat)

(6) (11) CBS News

(7) The Magic Carpet—Travel

(48) Mozart's Special—Concert

7:30

(2) Medical Report—Discussion

(4) Sports Digest—Discussion

(6) (11) Fit for Tomorrow—Exercise

8:00

(2) Movie—Drama (1976)
The Right Hand. Cybil builds a successful business from a nearly bankrupt store she inherited. Sue Spiegel, Jordan Miller. (2½ hrs.)

(4) Baseball
Chicago vs. Los Angeles

(5) Carol and Ted—Variety
Carol and Ted's guests are The Singing Six and comedian Harry Price.

(7) There She Goes—Comedy
Linda must decide between two new jobs. Linda Todd. (Repeat)

(10) Consumer Survival—Education

8:30

(6) (11) Nature's Country—Adventure
Tim Casey finds wounded mountain lion cub and brings it back to the ranch.

(7) Sargent Report—Discussion

(61) Movie—Mystery (1968)
Final Touchdown. A sports writer is murdered on Tolcan's football field. Richard Sharkey, Tony Musto, Rita Chu. (2 hrs.)

9:00

(6) (11) Movie—Musical (1978)
Dance Your Feet Off. Better-than-average tale of a young dance company's rise to fame. Good musical numbers. Sandy Kaplan, Eleanor Smith, Robert Nigro. (2 hrs.)

(7) Police Force—Mystery
Officer Dale captures leader of jewel-theft ring. Frank McNamara, Lena Johnson. (Repeat)

(10) Wall Street Review—Discussion

(48) Challenge for Life—Religion.

9:30

(5) José Garcia—Celebrities
Scheduled: Helen Wong, Chi-Chi, Angela Farber, George Garo, Sam Yak.

(10) News—Joseph Hovey

(48) The Family—Serial

Movie Schedule

A movie schedule is another kind of schedule that is printed in most newspapers every day. Most movie schedules look something like the one below.

Bijou: *The Spy Goes to France* — 11:00, 2:00, 4:30, 7:30, 9:15
Cinema 433: *Haunted Chambers* — 3:00, 4:45, 6:30, 8:00, 9:30;
    Dianna Jones — 5:30, 7:20, 9:10
Majestic: *Sing It Again* — 11:30, 1:30, 3:30, 5:30, 7:30, 9:30
Seashell: *Summer Romps* — 5:55, 7:30, 9:05, 10:45
Strand: *Get That Guy!* — 4:30, 6:00, 7:30, 9:00, 10:30
Warwick: *The Great Sweeney* — 5:30, 7:15, 9:30

A movie schedule lists the name of the theater, the name of the movie, and the time that each movie begins. If you want to know what a movie is about and who stars in it, you will have to look somewhere else. There usually are ads on the same page as the movie schedule. These ads may give you an idea of what the movie is about and who stars in it. Many newspapers print reviews that tell you what the movie is about. They also tell you what the reviewer liked or didn't like about the movie.

Now look again at the movie schedule. The first theater listed is the Bijou. What is the name of the movie playing there? *The Spy Goes to France* is the name of the movie. How many times in a day is it being shown? That's right. It is being shown five times. The movie starts at 11:00 A.M. and at 2:00, 4:30, 7:30, and 9:15 P.M. Notice that A.M. and P.M. are not used after the times. The times a movie is shown are listed in order. Most movies are only shown in the afternoon and evening, but sometimes a movie may be shown in the morning. So you need to use common sense to tell whether the first time listed is A.M. or P.M.

Like a television guide, a movie schedule can help you plan your time. Let's say that you have to be home by

9:45 at night. You want to see the movie at the Bijou, the theater just down the street. If you went to the 7:30 show, would you be home in time? Since the next show at the Bijou starts at 9:15, you know that you would leave the theater before that time.

Baseball Schedule

Another schedule often printed in a newspaper is that of the local baseball team's games. Below is the July schedule for the Pittsburgh Pirates, a National League baseball team. Notice that the schedule looks like a calendar. On each day that the Pirates play, the location of the team they are playing is printed in that square. You can see that the Pirates do not play every day of the month.

PIRATES SCHEDULE				All times Pittsburgh time / Shaded areas home games / TV Channel 2		
SUN	MON	TUES	WED	THURS	FRI	SAT
July		1	2	3 / Chi / (2:30)	4 / Chi / (8:30-TV)	5 / NY / (2:00-TV)
6 / NY / (2:00-TV)	7 / Cinn / (7:30)	8 / Cinn / (7:30)	9 / Cinn / (7:30)	10	11 / St. L / (8:30-TV)	12 / St. L / (8:30-TV)
13 / St. L / (2:30-TV)	14 / Chi / (8:30-TV)	15 / Chi / (2:30-TV)	16 / Phila / (6:00)	17 / Phila / (2:00-TV)	18 / Phila / (7:30)	19 / San D. / (2:00-TV)
20 / San D. / (2:00-TV)	21	22	23 / NY / (7:30-TV)	24 / NY / (7:30-TV)	25 / Cinn / (2:30-TV)	26 / Cinn / (8:35-TV)
27 / Cinn / (8:35-TV)	28 / St. L / (7:30)	29 / St. L / (2:00)	30	31		

Now read the information at the top of the schedule. What does a shaded square tell you? Yes, it tells you the games that will be played at the home ball park in Pittsburgh. What does a white square tell? It tells you the games that will be played away — in the other team's ball park. Some of the baseball games are shown on television. You could watch those games on channel 2.

Now look at Thursday, July 3. Which team are the Pirates playing? That's right. The Pirates are playing the National League team from Chicago, the Cubs. The time of the game is shown in parentheses. Notice that A.M. and P.M. are not listed after the time. Most games are played in the afternoon and evening. Is the July 3 game going to be played in Pittsburgh or Chicago? Yes, the game will be played in Chicago.

Look at the game scheduled for July 5. What time does this game start? That's right, at 2:00. Would you be able to watch this game on television? Yes, after the time, "TV" is printed. By watching channel 2, you could see this game. Is this game going to be played in Pittsburgh? The shaded square tells you that this game will be a home game and will be played in Pittsburgh.

Now use the TV guide, the movie schedule, and the baseball schedule to answer the following items. Use a separate piece of paper. Write the number of each item and the letter of the correct answer.

1. According to the TV guide, one of the stars of the 9:00 movie, *Dance Your Feet Off*, is
   a. Linda Todd.   c. Sue Spiegel.
   b. Sandy Kaplan.   d. Harry Price.

2. According to the TV guide, which is the right listing for an adventure show?
   a. Channel 48 at 9:00   c. Channels 6 and 11 at 8:30
   b. Channel 7 at 8:00   d. Channel 7 at 9:00

3. Tonight at 7:00, Rona is going to watch "Mozart's Special" on channel 48. At 8:30, she wants to watch the mystery movie, *Final Touchdown*. Will she be able to watch all of "Mozart's Special" before seeing *Final Touchdown*?
   a. Yes   c. You can't tell by reading
   b. No   the TV guide.

4. Look at the movie schedule. At which times is *Sing It Again* being shown?
- a. 11:30, 1:30, 3:30, 5:00, 7:30, 9:00
- b. 7:30, 9:15
- c. 11:30, 1:30, 3:30, 5:30, 7:30, 9:30
- d. 11:00, 7:30, 9:30

5. Ed and Sarah are going out to dinner. They will be finished eating by 9:15. It takes them ten minutes to get to any of the theaters. According to the movie schedule, which movies will they be able to see on time without having to wait for more than half an hour?
- a. *The Spy Goes to France, Sing It Again, The Great Sweeney*
- b. All of the movies except *Get That Guy!*
- c. *The Spy Goes to France, Summer Romps*
- d. *Haunted Chambers, Sing It Again, The Great Sweeney*

6. Look at the baseball schedule. On which date(s) do the Pirates play a game against the New York Mets in New York?
- a. July 5 and 6
- b. July 10
- c. July 23 and 24
- d. July 22

7. According to the baseball schedule, at what time will the Pirates play a game against the Philadelphia Phillies that will be shown on television?
- a. 2:30
- b. 6:00
- c. 7:30
- d. 2:00

8. Bertha is going to visit Larry in Pittsburgh from July 11 to 17. Larry wants to take Bertha to a Pirates' home game. Which team or teams would Bertha and Larry be able to see the Pirates play?
- a. Philadelphia Phillies only
- b. St. Louis Cardinals and Chicago Cubs
- c. St. Louis Cardinals, Chicago Cubs, and Philadelphia Phillies

A Mother in Mannville

by Marjorie Kinnan Rawlings

The orphanage is high in the Carolina mountains. I went there in the autumn to be alone to do some troublesome writing. I wanted mountain air to blow out the sickness I had gotten from staying too long in the subtropics. And I was homesick for the turning of the maples in October, for the corn shocks and pumpkins and black walnut trees. I found them all around a cabin that belonged to the orphanage. When I took the cabin, which was half a mile beyond the orphanage farm, I asked for somebody to chop wood for the fireplace.

Late one afternoon, I looked up, a little startled, from my typewriter. A boy stood at the door. My pointer dog, my companion, was at his side and had not barked to warn me that someone was there. The boy was probably twelve years old but undersized. He wore overalls, a torn shirt, and was barefoot. He said, "I'm Jerry. I can chop some wood today."

"You? But you're too small."

"Size doesn't matter for chopping wood," he said. "Some of the big boys don't chop wood very well. I've been chopping wood at the orphanage a long time."

"Very well, there's the ax. See what you can do." I went back to work, and he began to chop. The blows were rhythmic and steady. Shortly I had forgotten him, the sound no more of an interruption than a constant rain. I suppose an hour and a half passed before I heard the boy's steps on the cabin stoop.

"I have to go to supper now," he said. "I can come again tomorrow."

I said, "I'll pay you now for what you've done," thinking I should probably have to insist on an older boy. We went together to the back of the cabin. A large amount of solid wood had been cut. "But you've done as much as an adult," I said. "This is a splendid pile."

I looked at him, actually, for the first time. His hair was the color of the corn shocks; his eyes, very direct, were like the gray mountain sky when it was about to rain, with a shadowing of blue. I gave him a dollar. "You may come tomorrow afternoon," I said, "and thank you very much."

He looked at me and at the dollar and seemed to want to speak, but could not, and turned away.

At daylight, I was half wakened by the sound of chopping. It was so even in sound that I went back to sleep. When I left my bed, the boy had gone, and a stack of kindling was neatly piled against the cabin wall. He came again after school and worked until it was time to return to the orphanage.

Jerry had been at the orphanage since he was four. I could picture him at four, with the same serious gray-blue eyes and the same — independence? No, the word that comes to me is *rightfulness*. It is based on courage, but it is more than bravery. It is honest, but it is more than honesty.

The ax handle broke one day. Jerry said the orphanage woodshop would repair it. I brought money to pay for the job, and he refused it. "I'll pay for it," he said. "I broke it. I brought the ax down carelessly."

"But no one hits accurately every time," I told him. "The fault was in the handle."

It was only then that he would take the money. He was willing to pay for his own carelessness. He tried to do careful work; and if he failed, he took the responsibility.

And he did for me the unnecessary things, the gracious things, that we find done only by the great of heart — things no training can teach, for they are done out of natural thoughtfulness. He found a cubbyhole beside the fireplace that I had not noticed. There, on his own, he put wood so that it would be dry in case of sudden chilly weather. He noticed that a stone was loose in the rough walk to the cabin. He dug a deeper hole and steadied the stone, although he came to the house by a shortcut over the bank.

I found that when I tried to return his thoughtfulness with such things as candy and apples, he was wordless. "Thank you" was, perhaps, an expression for which he had had no use, for his courtesy was natural. He only looked at the gift and at me, and I saw deep in his clear eyes gratitude and affection.

He became very friendly with my pointer, Pat. There is a strong relationship between a child and a dog. Perhaps they have the same singleness of spirit, the same kind of wisdom. It is difficult to explain, but it exists.

When I went across the state for a weekend, I left the dog in Jerry's charge. Fog filled the mountain passes so dangerously that it was Monday noon before I returned to the cabin. The dog had been fed and cared for that morning. Jerry came early in the afternoon, worried. "The superintendent said nobody would drive in the fog," he said. "I came last night, and you hadn't come. So I brought Pat some of my breakfast this morning. I wouldn't have let anything happen to him."

I gave him two dollars in payment, and he looked at the bills and went away. But that night he came in the darkness and knocked at the door. "Come in, Jerry," I said, "if you're allowed to be out this late."

"I told the supervisor — maybe a story — that I thought you would want to see me," he said.

"That's true," I assured him, and saw his relief. "I want to hear about how you managed with the dog."

He sat by the fire with me and told me of their two days together. The dog lay close to him and found a comfort there that I did not have for him. "He stayed right with me," he told me, "except when he ran into the bushes. There was a place where the grass was high, and I lay down in it and hid. I could hear Pat hunting for me. When he found me, he acted crazy; he ran around and around me, in circles."

We watched the flames.

"That's an apple log," he said. "It burns the prettiest of any wood."

We were very close, and he suddenly felt like talking.

"You look a little bit like my mother," he said. "Especially in the dark, by the fire."

"You have remembered how she looked, all these years?"

"My mother lives in Mannville," he said.

I did not know why finding that he had a mother so greatly disturbed me. Then I understood my distress. I was upset that any parent would go away and leave a child — especially a son like this one. The orphanage was a wholesome place; the food was more than adequate. Granted, perhaps, the children felt no lack. But what parent could leave such a son as this one?

"Have you seen her, Jerry — lately?" I asked.

"I see her every summer. She sends for me."

I wanted to cry out, "Why are you not with her? How can she let you go away again?"

He said, "She comes up here from Mannville whenever she can. She doesn't have a job now."

His face shone in the firelight. "She wanted to give me

a puppy, but no one can keep a puppy here. You remember the suit I had on last Sunday?" He was plainly proud. "She sent me that for Christmas. The Christmas before that," he drew a long breath, enjoying the memory, "she sent me a pair of roller skates. I let the other boys use them; they're careful of them."

She had not, then, entirely deserted or forgotten him. But what circumstance other than poverty . . . ?

"I'm going to take the two dollars you gave me for taking care of Pat," he said, "and buy her a pair of gloves."

I hated her. Poverty or not, there was other food than bread, and the heart could starve as quickly as the body. He was taking his money to buy gloves for her, and she lived away from him, in Mannville, and contented herself with sending him skates.

"She likes white gloves," he said. "Do you think I can get them for two dollars?"

"I think so," I said.

We did not speak of Jerry's mother again. His having a mother, any sort, relieved me of the ache I had had about him. He was not lonely. It was none of my concern.

He came every day and cut my wood and did small helpful favors. The days had become cold, and often I asked him to come inside the cabin. He would lie on the floor in front of the fire, with one arm across Pat, and they would both doze and wait quietly for me to finish work. Other days, they ran with a common delight through the fields, and he brought me back bright red maple leaves and golden-yellow chestnut boughs.

I was ready to go. I said to him, "You have been my good friend, Jerry. I shall miss you. Pat will miss you too. I am leaving tomorrow." He did not answer, and I watched him go in silence.

I expected him the next day, but he did not come. Late in the day, I stopped by the orphanage and left the cabin key with Miss Clark.

"And will you call Jerry for me so I can say good-by to him?"

"I don't know where he is," she said. "I'm afraid he's

not well. He didn't eat his dinner this noon. One of the other boys saw him running up the hill into the fields."

I was almost relieved; it would be easier not to say good-by.

I said, "I wanted to talk with you about his mother — why he's here — but I'm in more of a hurry than I expected. Here's some money. I'd like you to buy things for him at Christmas and on his birthday. It will be better than for me to try to send him things. I could so easily duplicate — skates, for instance."

She blinked her honest eyes. "There's not much use for skates here," she said.

Her response annoyed me.

"What I mean," I said, "is that I don't want to duplicate the things his mother sends him. I might have chosen skates if I didn't know she had already given them to him."

She stared at me.

"I don't understand," she said. "He has no mother. He has no skates."

THE MYSTERY OF OAK ISLAND

by Dale Titler

Every buried treasure has a strange history, and the Oak Island treasure is one of the most mysterious. Tiny Oak Island lies just beyond Nova Scotia's coast. Oak Island is one of the 365 islands in Mahone Bay.

The secret of Oak Island has cost seven lives and wasted over six million dollars. Every search for the treasure for the past 182 years has failed. Even today, no one knows just what is buried there: pirate gold, the French crown jewels, Viking supplies, or the remains of a lost civilization. Many people agree that it is the most perfectly buried treasure in the world.

From the book *UNNATURAL RESOURCES: True Stories of American Treasures* by Dale M. Titler. © 1973 by Dale M. Titler. Published by Prentice-Hall, Inc., Englewood Cliffs, New Jersey.

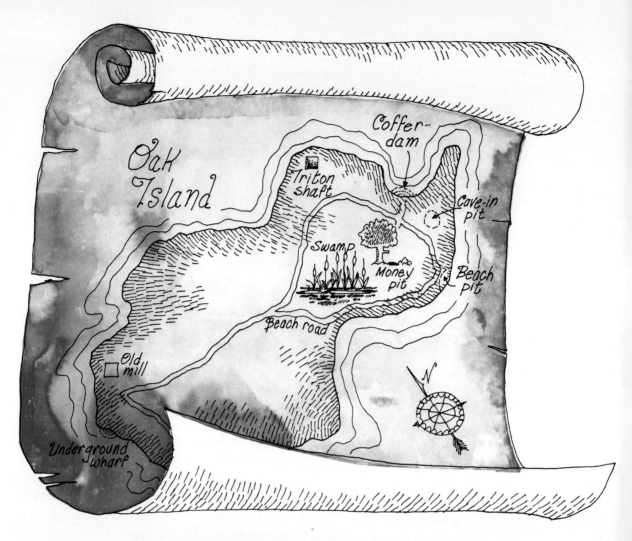

The place of the treasure was first discovered in 1795, when three teen-age boys beached their canoe on Oak Island. On a hill near the shore, they found a giant oak tree with a sawed-off limb sticking straight out from its trunk. The limb had been dead for a long time. But it still showed signs of deep cuts — perhaps from a heavy rope. Under the sawed-off limb, the boys discovered a round hollow in the ground. It looked as if the earth had settled after something had been buried there. These clues could mean only one thing: Something heavy had been lowered into the ground with a rope wrapped around the limb. *Was it a pirate chest?*

The next day, the boys returned to the island with shovels and picks. Ten feet down, they hit something hard. It was a platform of rough oak boards, six inches thick. *Did it protect the treasure?* They removed the boards and dug on, day after day. At twenty feet and at thirty feet, they found the wooden boards again.

The boys were very tired from their long hard work, and an early winter sent them back home to Nova Scotia. When they asked old-timers about Oak Island, they were told a story of bad luck. Fifty years ago, ships had landed there, and strange noises had sounded across Mahone Bay. One night, two men who were out fishing rowed close enough to the island to see people outlined by the light of roaring bonfires. The men went ashore to find out what was happening and were never seen again.

This tale fired the boys' hopes of recovering the treasure, but they could find no one to help them. Years later, one of them interested a local doctor, John Lynds, in the undertaking. As the Oak Island Treasure Company, they raised money, hired a small crew, and brought tools to the island. In 1803, the crew began digging.

Every ten feet, oak boards delayed the digging. The crew also found layers of coconut matting, charcoal, and ship's putty. At ninety feet, they uncovered a new puzzle. They found a flat stone, a yard long and sixteen inches wide, covered with strange markings. No one at that time could understand the markings, and the stone passed from hand to hand. Over one hundred years later, a teacher of languages was able to break the code. The markings on the stone said, "Beneath this stone, two million pounds are buried." In 1928, the stone was used as a doorstop in a Halifax office. But since that time, no one has seen it.

Lynds's crew, excited by the discovery, dug deeper. At ninety-seven feet below the surface, a worker pushed a metal rod three feet into the wet ground and struck wood. Lynds was sure that this was the last set of oak boards before the treasure. Also, it was getting dark. So he ordered the work stopped until the next workday. But when the crew returned to work, they found that water had filled the hole! They pumped out the water for weeks, but an underground stream filled the pit as fast as they emptied it. Winter came and all work stopped.

The next summer, Lynds's crew dug a new hole to the north of the flooded "treasure pit." At one hundred ten feet into the second hole, three workers began to tunnel across toward the treasure. They hoped to reach the treasure and be below the water line. As their shovels broke through the last few feet of dirt, tons of water burst suddenly into the new hole. The workers escaped, and the water rose to sixty feet. Lynds's crew had to give up the search.

About forty years later, still remembering his near success, Lynds tried again. His crew used a crude horsepower pod drill and hit a wooden container at one hundred feet. When they raised the drill, they found three pieces of gold chain in its pod, or bit. A shout went up. They had hit the treasure!

When the crew looked closely at the gold pieces and wood shavings, they felt sure that the treasure was stored in oak chests or barrels. Only seventy-five feet of water separated them from the treasure now!

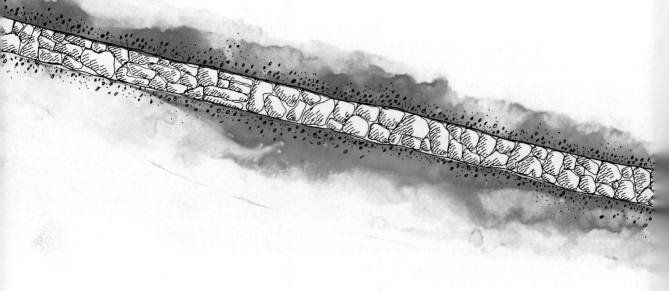

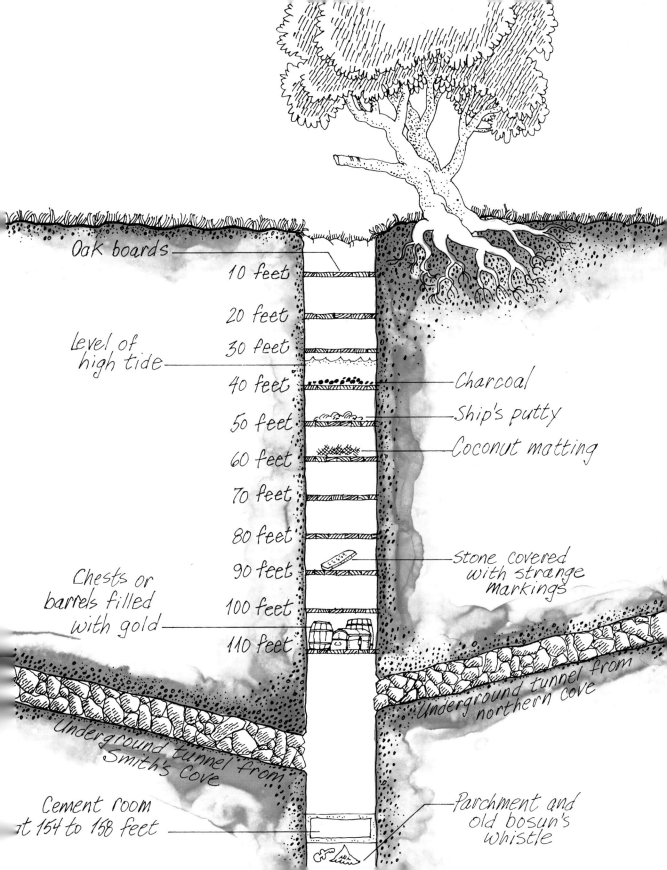

Oak boards

10 feet

20 feet

Level of high tide

30 feet

40 feet — Charcoal

50 feet — Ship's putty

60 feet — Coconut matting

70 feet

80 feet

90 feet — Stone covered with strange markings

Chests or barrels filled with gold

100 feet

110 feet

Underground tunnel from northern cove

Underground tunnel from Smith's Cove

Cement room at 154 to 158 feet

Parchment and old bosun's whistle

Because the flood water was salty, the workers believed that the pits were connected to the ocean. They searched the northern cove, which was about five hundred feet away. There they found five well-hidden intakes that let the Atlantic Ocean flow into the pits. Now the crew was certain a wonderful treasure was buried. *Why else would anyone go to so much trouble to protect it?*

Lynds's workers built a dam to hold the ocean back. But the strong tide forced it apart. Then they dug a hole over one hundred feet deep on the south side of the treasure pit. But as the workers tunneled toward the treasure, water again burst through. Lynds and his crew gave up again.

A few years later, a third company tried to recover the treasure by blocking the tunnels that flooded the treasure pit, but that company failed also. Over the next ten years, two more companies lost over seventy thousand dollars trying to reach the treasure.

In 1893, Frederick Blair, a Nova Scotia merchant, formed a new Oak Island Treasure Company. Blair's workers reopened the first hole and widened it. A steam drill reached deep into the hole and found a "room" seven feet deep and five feet square. The samples of material that the drill brought up were looked at closely. Blair's crew learned that the material was an early kind of hand-mixed cement.

They continued to drill and discovered such unusual things as a tiny ball of parchment with *w* and *i* written in black ink and a tiny, carved-bone bosun's whistle, shaped like a violin.

But the water coming from the intakes at the northern cove still kept the workers from the big treasure. They tried to stop the water from coming into the treasure pit. Blair's crew drilled fifty holes near the edge of the water. Then they made the holes larger with dynamite. The crew hoped that the holes would fill with water but that the treasure pit would dry out. But all the holes filled with water, and the treasure pit was still flooded. To find out where the stream of water began, Blair poured red dye into the treasure pit. When no dye appeared at the northern cove, the workers were puzzled. But on the south side of the island, at Smith's Cove, the red dye stained the beach. There was not *one* tunnel guarding the treasure — there were *two!*

The work went on for four more years. New pits were dug, one as deep as one hundred sixty feet. When Blair's company folded in 1897, he was still sure that he could reach the treasure. He bought out his partners, raised more money, and kept digging — all for nothing. Finally, in 1903, he gave up.

In 1909, young Franklin Roosevelt, who was to become the President of the United States, and three friends raised five thousand dollars to dig on Oak Island. They believed the pit contained the crown jewels of France. But when winter came, they, too, went home defeated.

Fifteen years later, Gilbert Heddon, from New Jersey, decided to recover the treasure. He bought land on the island and hired a mining and drilling company. His crew laid underwater electric cables from the mainland for their lighting and high-speed pumps. They cleared out the treasure pit to one hundred fifty-five feet, but after five years, they had to give up.

World War II put a stop to treasure hunts, but when it was over, new treasure seekers arrived at Oak Island every summer. Since the first pit was begun 182 years ago, over six million dollars have been poured into more than fifty water-filled holes on the island. More than twenty well-planned hunts for the treasure have failed.

Who thought of this grand puzzle? No one really knows. The people who buried the treasure, hidden so perfectly that present-day tools can't uncover it, still hold the secret.

Diaries Are for Secrets

by Ruth E. Hampton

Celia was still fuming as she hopped off her bicycle and picked up a can from beside the highway. Mom had just given her another talk — all because she was caught reading her sister Merrilee's diary.

Dear Diary, Joan thinks I should dye my hair. . . . Dear Diary, I think David likes me. . . . Dear . . .

Naturally, Mom took Merrilee's side. "Why can't you be more like your sister, Celia?" she had asked. "Other girls don't spend their lives riding a bicycle or walking in ditches. Other girls keep diaries of their own instead of reading their sister's. Other girls . . ."

Wouldn't her family laugh if she admitted she was trying to help clean up the world! Picking up trash might not be her family's idea of a job, but Celia had saved over twenty dollars from gathering cans and bottles. It sure beat baby-sitting. She'd do anything rather than baby-sit.

Maybe today would be the day the red-tail hawk's eggs hatched. She pedaled hard, turning up the canyon road in a cloud of dust.

The nest, high in a double-topped pine at the foot of the hill, didn't show from the road. Celia hid her bike and ran up the hillside until she was level with the nest. A hawk flew out of the tree, leaving the untidy cradle of sticks looking flat and empty. Only when the breeze lifted the blanket of feathers could Celia see the flash of white eggs.

Her eyes ached from squinting, but one of the eggs seemed to be moving among the sticks and fluff. She climbed up a juniper tree to get a better look. It wasn't an egg. It was a tiny white ghost of a bird with black, staring eyes. When it disappeared, Celia pulled a note-book from her pocket. Balanced against the juniper, she wrote: *April 14. 3:30 P.M. Casper — No. 1 nestling.*

The next week, two more fluffy ghosts appeared in the nest. Celia named them Spook and Phantom.

After school on Monday, Celia hurried into her jeans and pedaled the two miles to the canyon. Each hour she was away, she worried that someone would find the hawks. A green truck passed her on the dirt road, so she casually coasted past the place where she usually hid her bike. Later she wrote: *April 21. Possibly 4 babies. Looks like Casper pecks others. Cold! Adult flew down with something in talons. Feeding?* Celia stared at the fara-way nest. She wished she dared to ask for Dad's field glasses.

The next Saturday, she rode out to the shopping center and found a pair of low-priced binoculars — $22.95, seven power. She rushed outside the store and, pedaling her way through the traffic, hurried to the canyon. Her money was gone, but she hadn't been forced to tell about the nest of hawks.

On the hillside, she unwrapped the glasses and read the instructions: "Cover left eye, adjust right eyepiece. . . . Cover right eye, adjust . . . " It worked. She was staring at a pine branch that appeared inches instead of yards away. It took practice, but Celia found the nest in time to

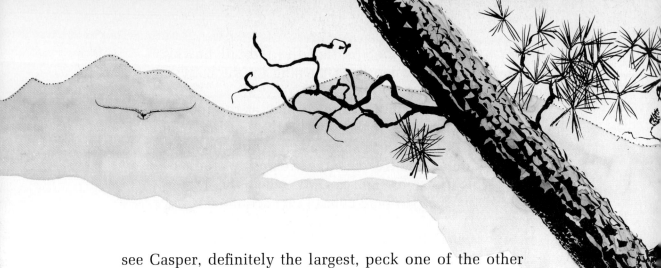

see Casper, definitely the largest, peck one of the other nestlings. When Casper settled back and closed its eyes, a fly moved down its dark, curved beak.

The bird book said that a hawk's eye may be eight times sharper than a human's. That meant the hawk screaming overhead could see Celia a little better than she was seeing it. Swinging back to the nest, she definitely counted four young. She named the fourth one Shadow. In her notebook, she wrote: *April 23. Casper is getting small spots on its wings. Others still white. Shadow No. 4.*

May 1. Overcast. Babies are fed mice, moles, gophers. Parents tear up meat, bone, hair, and poke it down throats.

May 2. Today when I started up the hill, the parents both came screaming over my head. The little ones froze. Didn't move once in twenty minutes. When I left, the darker, heavier female (?) flew over and screamed, "All clear."

May 9. Couldn't go to nest. Green truck in canyon.

May 12. Casper looks pinkish, others dirty gray.

May 16. Boys in yellow car with gun, hunting.

May 20. Casper and Spook have feathers just alike. Same age, maybe same sex? They bully little ones.

May 26. One of the younger ones almost fell out of nest. Went down over the side. Had to scramble back. The stupid parents just watched.

One Friday when Celia arrived at the pine tree, the nest looked empty. Worried, she searched the lower

limbs and ground. Then a slight movement above the nest caught her eye. Perched on a branch was one youngster, looking like the adult birds except for having a slightly lighter color. The other two feathered ones were on perches too. Shadow, still downy, was lying low in the nest.

June 3. Today was wing-stretching day. All four were up, two on nest, two above. Parent brought gopher, and they mobbed her, pecking and flapping.

June 4. Casper was up in a branch crying out loud when the boys drove by. I stood still so the adults wouldn't see me and scream. Green truck went by again.

June 7. Casper was gone. Thought boys had shot it, but it was staring at me from another tree. Golden with small spots.

Several days later, Celia hid the binoculars under her shirt. Then she climbed on her bicycle and pedaled slowly to the canyon. School was out. It was almost time for the young hawks to fly away. Even if the parents came back to the nest next year, it wouldn't be the same. Never again would she watch the lives of Casper, Spook, Phantom, and Shadow together as a family.

She smiled, remembering how they had looked like little ghosts at first, peering over the edge. The smile faded. Was growing up always hurting, leaving, losing? Merrilee was growing up, Mom had said. That's why she'd rather go on dates and keep secret diaries than do things with her own sister. Well, Celia had a secret diary too — a hawk diary.

The sudden roar of a motor sent Celia into the ditch. The yellow car was racing toward her, and from the window, a gun pointed at the sky. She looked up and saw one of the hawks going into its dive to warn off the intruders and cry "freeze" to its young.

"No! No!" Celia was screaming as the car skidded to a halt, and the boy steadied for a shot. She hurled herself off the bike to try to stop him, but she was thrown backward as the shot rang out. The binoculars flew out from under her shirt and came down on her mouth. The sky went black.

Celia woke up to the taste of blood and the sight of a blue work shirt blotting out the world. Celia moaned, "The red tail. They shot the red tail."

"They missed him. It's okay. Are you all right? Looks like a broken tooth is the worst of it." The woman bending over her motioned to her young helper. "Daryl, give me a hand." They loaded Celia's bike into the back of the green truck, then helped her into the cab. "Hasn't anybody told you to wear binoculars under your arm?" the woman asked. When Celia didn't answer, she went on. "You must be a red-tail fan. Don't suppose you'd know where there is a nest, would you?"

Celia drew her tongue across the ragged sharpness of her tooth and once more said nothing.

"We've been trying to locate the nests so we can determine when the young hawks fly. So far this year, we haven't had one nest sighting for this area."

"Why? Do you shoot them too?" Celia pulled herself up and sat stiffly between the woman and her helper.

"No, not at all. We protect hawks. And we try not to start logging in hawk and eagle areas until the nestlings fly. What we need are some dates for this canyon."

Slowly, Celia pulled the note pad from her pocket. "Do you mean like this?"

Daryl flipped the pages. "Hmmm. Egg hatched the fourteenth of April. Dates, times, weather. Looks like they'll fly any day now. This is a well-kept diary...."

Celia reached for the pad and shuddered. "Oh, please," she said, "this isn't a diary; it's my notebook." She smiled a slightly crooked smile as she added, "Diaries are for secrets."

SMART ALEC: **What is the definition of *illegal*?**
CLEVER CLARA: **"A sick bird."**

FIFTEEN HONEST COINS

by Louise and Yuan-Hsi Kuo

This is one of the many tales about a magistrate named Pao Kung who lived during the Sung Dynasty. The law was carried out by him, whether a suspect was a high official or only a peasant. He was always just and honest.

In a little village away from the noise and rush of the city, there once lived a poor old woman and her son. Every day they arose before dawn to gather twigs from the nearby mountains. When the sun arose, the boy was already carrying the bundles to the marketplace while his mother returned to their thatched hut to attend to her duties. With the money from the firewood, he usually bought some oil, rice, vegetables and, once in a while, a few eggs or a very small amount of meat. By noon, he would be on his way home. Without exception, this was their daily simple way of life.

One morning when he went to the marketplace, there was the usual crowd bargaining, but nobody came to purchase his twigs. As he waited patiently, he suddenly caught sight of a small bag lying near his twigs. "Someone must have dropped it," he said to himself, and looking hastily into the bag, he saw some coins. Without waiting any longer, he hurried home.

"Why have you come back so early today?" his mother asked.

"I had good luck! I found this bag containing some coins. The firewood wasn't sold, but perhaps whatever is in the bag will make up for it," he replied.

The mother and son eagerly opened the bag to count the coins that amounted to fifteen in all.

"Someone must be very unhappy over the loss," she sighed. "My son, you must return this to the owner. He or she may need it — just like us — to buy rice and oil. The owner's family may even be starving," she added, trying to persuade him to hurry.

"But Ma, I've never seen the owner. To whom should I give the money?"

"Just stay at the same spot where you found the money and wait until someone comes looking for it. I don't feel right about keeping these coins. I insist that you go right now."

So he returned to the marketplace and stood there to watch the passing crowds. It was nearly noon, and the morning market was almost over when a merchant walked by. He turned his head in all directions as if searching for something.

"Good master! What are you looking for? Have you lost something?" asked the boy.

"Yes, I'm looking for a purse. I must have dropped it somewhere in the marketplace."

"Well then, is this yours?" the young fellow asked, holding out the bag.

"It certainly is!" the merchant exclaimed as he grabbed it and began counting the coins. "One, two, three, four, five . . . fifteen! Why — how is that — only fifteen! I had thirty coins in my purse," he shouted angrily. "You must have kept fifteen for yourself. How dare you return my purse with only half the money!"

"There were only fifteen coins. I'm an honest person. Really I am, truly, truly," the youth pleaded.

An argument started, and in no time at all, a big crowd gathered to hear what was happening. The argument went on endlessly, each accusing the other of dishonesty.

At last the crowd urged them to see Pao Kung, the magistrate. The whole procession followed them to the *yamen* where the two angry fellows were given a hearing.

"How many coins did you find in that bag?" the magistrate asked the youth.

"Fifteen."

"Did you count the coins by yourself?" the magistrate inquired.

"No, my mother and I opened the bag, and we counted them together."

Thereupon the magistrate asked an officer to fetch the mother instantly.

"How many coins did you count in the bag?" the magistrate questioned her.

"There were fifteen coins. I urged my son to go back to the same spot in the marketplace where he picked up the bag and wait for the owner so it could be returned."

The magistrate looked at the old woman and the youth from head to foot. After this appraisal, he asked the merchant, "How much money have you lost?"

"I lost thirty coins. That fellow returned only fifteen. He has kept fifteen. He is dishonest. I want my thirty coins," he yelled in a demanding voice.

The magistrate looked at the merchant from head to foot. After this scrutiny, a faint smile passed over his face. Then suddenly banging on the table for attention so that all could hear, he turned to the merchant and said, "Since you are sure that you have lost a purse with thirty coins, this bag with only fifteen coins is clearly not yours. Therefore, you cannot claim it."

Then addressing the youth, the magistrate said, "Since you found this bag with the fifteen coins and no one has claimed rightful ownership, you may keep it to buy some food for your old mother. The case is now closed."

Everyone in the courtroom felt satisfied with the wise, just decision of the magistrate.

Women Fighting Crime

by Michael Fooner

"We heard shots. The car radio came on and directed us to a building. Four men ran out, carrying shotguns. We jumped out of the car, guns drawn, and yelled, 'Freeze! Police! Drop your guns!' They stopped, and we got them up against the wall. We searched them, took them in, and booked them on charges of robbery and having weapons."

That sort of thing can happen any day in any city or town. It was different this time because one of the police officers taking part was a woman.

Her partner was a man, and when asked about what happened, he said, "She did her part, the way it was supposed to be done." Both officers got equal credit for "making a good collar." That group of words is police jargon, meaning "carrying out a good arrest of suspects of a serious crime."

Asked if her job is dangerous, Police Officer Parker — known as Alicia to her family and friends — says, "As a police officer, you're trained. You know what to do."

That kind of report could not have been made before 1900 because women were not allowed to be members of a police force until after that time. The first hiring of a woman as a *regular* police officer was in Stuttgart, Germany, in 1904. In the United States, the first female police officer was hired in Los Angeles in 1911. In London, Scotland Yard got its first regular woman police officer in 1915. In New York, women were hired to work in jails in the 1840's and to work as police station turnkeys in the 1880's, but these women were not looked upon as having regular police jobs. New York got its first regular policewomen in 1918. Because so many men were in the military service during World War I, (1914–1918), women were hired for police work. Since that time, a growing number of countries have hired women police officers.

While women and men police generally do the same things, women in some countries are given special duties. These duties often show the country's way of life.

In India, female police officers often work on crowd control at festivals, demonstrations, and strikes when large numbers of women take part. Another important job these police officers have is checking the belongings of female travelers to make sure that they are not taking illegal articles out of the country.

Control of auto traffic is the specialty of policewomen in Israel, where the traffic department is made up mostly of women. When women were first accepted for police work in Israel, they showed a special skill with traffic control and did so well that they became known as the best traffic officers in the world. They were asked to train traffic police in France, Great Britain, Japan, and many other countries. Because they did so well in traffic control, they were able to ask for other jobs in different branches of the department. Today, there are more women on the Israeli police force than in any other force in the world.

England was one of the first countries to give women patrol duty — an area that once belonged only to men. The Beat Constable Team was formed in England and is now used in other countries as well. It is a patrol system by teams of uniformed officers, with at least one female member on each team. When on patrol, the police officers get to know the people in the neighborhood. They listen to what the people have to say and watch for possible trouble. Besides working in the neighborhoods, the teams patrol airports, markets, and highways.

In many countries — such as France, England, Scotland, West Germany, and the United States — women play an important part in detective work. They gather information from all sorts of places and study it, help find criminals and victims, and find stolen goods. Usually they work in plain clothes. They go to the scene of a crime to get the facts. They question the people who saw the crime to get leads from them. But not all detectives work in plain clothes. Some work undercover, dressing and pretending to be criminals or possible victims. A New York City police officer named Kathleen has played the part of a housewife, Swedish nurse, and youth-gang member at different times to arrest drug pushers, purse snatchers, and robbers. Another officer, "Muggable Mary," made three hundred arrests in two years on the city streets.

Using women in detective work is an old idea that started before police departments were willing to accept them as regular officers. As early as 1893, Chicago had at least one woman assigned to help male detectives on difficult cases in which women and children were involved.

At one time, it might have seemed strange to see women on the police force. But today, the public in many parts of the world has become used to seeing women patrolling the city streets, directing traffic, doing detective work, and making arrests.

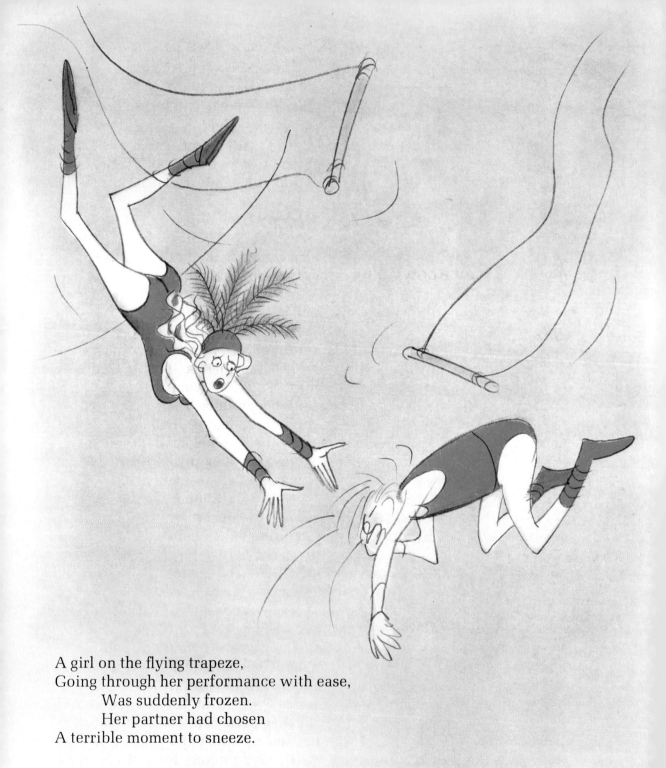

A girl on the flying trapeze,
Going through her performance with ease,
     Was suddenly frozen.
     Her partner had chosen
A terrible moment to sneeze.

Edward S. Mullins

60

Fetch!

by Robb White

The last thing George Dixon expected, or wanted, to meet in an apartment on the seventeenth floor was this huge Great Dane with an old tennis ball in his mouth. When Professor Werner called, "Come on in," and George opened the door, the only thing that greeted him was that dog who knocked him back against the wall.

"Play with the dog, Dixon. I'll be out in a minute," the professor said from somewhere in the apartment.

With that dog, you did what that dog wanted you to do: throw the ball so he could go galloping around and bring it back to you.

George had a lot more on his mind than playing with a dog. Six of his friends in Werner's archeology class already had tried to get the job. All had been turned down. Now it was his turn, and he wanted to rehearse his speech. But this dog was jumping all over him and the furniture, dropping the drool-soaked tennis ball on his best clothes.

Then the idea came. George took the slimy ball and held it up. "O.K., Fido, you're so smart; go get this one."

Instead of throwing the ball, George rolled it gently across the floor. Then with great satisfaction, he watched it roll under a low chest placed in front of an open window. The Great Dane bounded across the room, his tail knocking a vase of flowers off a table.

The dog did not stop, nor even slow down. With sudden horror, George watched him leap from the floor. He cleared the top of the chest and went on, stretched out, flying. Outside a gentle rain was lit by the streetlights far below. The huge dog sailed out into the rainy darkness. For what seemed a century to George, the body of the dog seemed to float in the air. Then it slowly sank out of sight, falling down through the rain.

The Great Dane did not make a sound as he fell toward the pavement, seventeen stories down.

For a moment, George just sat there, frozen with fear for the dog. Then George was on his feet running, looking only at the open, dark, and empty window.

Someone grabbed his arm, stopping him in mid-stride and spinning him around. "Come on!" Professor Werner said. "I'm late for a date, so we'll talk in the elevator."

"Wait!" George begged, trying to pull his arm free.

"Come on!" the professor ordered, yanking him to the door.

"No! Wait!" George said, but the professor pulled him out of the room and locked the door. Without a word, Werner dragged George to the elevator, shoved him into it, and pushed the button for the lobby.

It was only after the elevator began to sink that George really understood the very great size of the thing. He could still picture that beautiful dog sailing out into the darkness and almost feel the long, dreadful fall. Some of the windows the dog would fall past would have lights in them, some would be dark. The pavement would be wet with rain.

Slowly George realized that the professor had been talking to him all the time. They were going to dig in a faraway cave in Kurdistan, Turkey. They might find gold artifacts of some value. They might find clues to the missing chapters in the history of civilization.

George couldn't listen to the professor, couldn't pay attention. All George could think about was that great dog with the ball in his mouth, leaping so happily around the room. All he could think of was those huge, soft eyes asking George to throw the ball again — and the dirty trick he had pulled on the dog.

The professor kept talking and talking. It would be rugged in Kurdistan and dangerous. They would explore a cave with a deep hole in the floor, perhaps a thousand feet deep. Down this hole, some prehistoric person may have fallen fifty thousand years ago.

The dog had fallen *now*, tonight.

Slowly, as the elevator dial went past ten and nine and eight, George tried to erase the picture of that dog. He tried to think about himself — this job he wanted so badly, this meeting with Werner on which everything depended.

Had it been his fault? A dog had made a mistake and leaped out an open window. Had that been his fault? Was he to blame for that? Did he have to admit it? Should he lose this job because of a dog?

George realized slowly that the professor had been asking him a direct question. The elevator dial read three.

"Dixon," the professor asked again, "what is your definition of courage?"

It took all of George's mental strength to force his mind to pay attention. "Courage, sir? . . . Er . . . Courage? . . . I guess it's doing the right thing when you don't have to, even though no one is watching. Nobody sees anything."

Werner laughed. "That's a definition I'd never thought of. But it's not bad. Anyway, this expedition you and I are going on is going to take a lot of it."

"You and I." That's what he'd said. *"You and I."*

People would be standing in the rain now, looking down at that beautiful dog lying crushed on the wet pavement.

The elevator stopped, and the doors slid open silently. As Werner started out, George pushed the CLOSE DOORS button and then turned and put both hands on Werner's shoulders, pushing him back against the wall.

"I killed your dog," George said.

Werner stared at him.

"I was playing with the dog. Throwing the ball. He went out the window — just out — into the rain."

Werner said nothing as he pushed George's hands aside and then walked to the front of the elevator and pushed the seventeen button. The elevator going up made no sound at all. Werner stood in silence with his back to George.

"He was a beautiful dog," George said. "I'm sorry."

Werner said nothing as the doors opened and he stepped out. Without looking at George or waiting for him, Werner walked down the silent hall. He stopped outside his door, unlocked it, reached in, and turned on the lights. Then, at last, he turned and waited for George.

Feeling sick and seeing again that dark, open window, George walked slowly into the room. A great moving weight struck him from behind, knocking him flat on his face. For a moment, George just wanted to lie there, his face down on the carpet, his body waiting for more of the attack he knew he deserved.

Then something gently nudged him, and he turned his head. There was the Great Dane with that soggy tennis ball in his mouth, his tail wagging away, knocking things off a table.

"It was a mean thing to do to you, Dixon," Werner said. "But I need to know what sort of man I'm taking on this dangerous expedition."

George put his arms around the dog's neck and then got to his feet.

"There's a balcony outside that window," Werner said, smiling. "And this mutt loves to show off."

ICE STAR ON THE RISE

by Louis Sabin

Reggie Stanley glides toward the center of the ice, building up speed. The blades of his skates flash like silver knives, picking up the rays of a spotlight tracking him across the smooth surface. All at once Reggie lifts off. His arms reach out and his legs stretch wide in a midair giant step. Like a spring, he whirls two-and-a-half times in space before coming back to the ice.

Reggie lands lightly on his right skate, moving backward. The sound of clapping hands around the arena rings in the air. The takeoff, the leap, and the landing are perfect. But Reggie doesn't even smile at the sound of the clapping. His mind is totally on his performance, which has just begun. He skates on, drawing more applause, until his routine is over. Then the trim, five-foot-three-inch teen-ager leaves the ice.

It has all taken one minute, a minute packed with beauty and excitement. Now Reggie can rest. His face shows the joy he feels at the crowd's applause, and his smile matches the one worn by his coach, Donald Laws.

Someone shakes Reggie's hand and says, "You make everything look so easy."

"I guess the jumps and spins *do* look easy to anyone who doesn't know figure skating. They're *supposed* to look that way," Reggie answers as he bends to untie his skates. "But each routine is put together by my coach, who spends about a month on it. Then Coach Laws gives it to me, and I spend about six weeks getting the routine just right for competition. Believe me," he adds, laughing, "it's hard work."

Among Reggie's long string of ice triumphs are the 1974 Eastern and national beginner championships and the 1975 United States men's beginner title. Although his hopes for the national junior men's crown and the international competitions were crushed by several ankle injuries, he isn't discouraged. "That's the kind of setback you've got to expect," Reggie says. "But I'll be ready for the next senior men's competition. There are world championships every year. And, of course, I look forward to the 1980 Olympics — if I'm good enough."

To be good enough means keeping up with a heavy practice schedule on top of the normal demands of studying for school. Reggie explains, "The way things are, skating and school don't leave much free time. For example, my normal day goes like this: Get out of bed at 5:45 A.M., eat breakfast, then go down to the rink for an hour of practice. Skaters call it 'patch time.' It's called that because each skater practices on just a small section, or patch, of ice.

"After practice, there's school till 2:30 P.M. Some days, I head back to the rink after school. Other days, I go home to do some homework before going to practice again. When I go straight to the rink, I skate from three to eight o'clock, with a few rest periods. Then I go home to eat dinner, do homework, and go to bed. On good days, I get to watch a little TV.

"The schedule is even tougher during the competitive season, December through February. I have to travel, compete, practice, and squeeze in reading and other studies so I don't fall behind at school."

Reggie didn't put on a pair of ice skates until he was nine years old — late to begin a career in figure skating. "I liked skating right away, even though I was falling all the time. I wasn't one of those storybook successes, where the skater gets out on the ice and instantly is jumping and spinning like a professional. But skating really got to me.

The feeling of the ice under my blades was like skimming over glass. By the end of my first two-hour session, I could skate all the way around the rink without holding on to the railing.

"My skating improved over the next two years, and when I was eleven, I started taking lessons and practicing seriously. The lessons and practice weren't much fun. I kept wishing the sport would be just skating the way I felt inside. But I saw there was a lot more to skating than I could teach myself, and I wanted to get better. I also wanted to compete — and win. Well, all that practicing paid off when I won my first competition at eleven. That encouraged me to work harder, and I've been lucky enough to keep on winning."

Reggie accepts the sacrifices he must make in his search for skating honors. "Giving up some things is part of the deal you make with yourself," he says. "I mean, I've wanted to quit skating a few times. Then I could spend more time with friends and do a lot of the things I can't do now — like other sports, photography, woodworking, and, most of all, fishing. Still, you can't do everything. Success at figure skating makes up for the bad times and the sacrifices."

Skating, to Reggie, is more than winning medals and fame. "While I'm out there performing," he explains, "I sometimes look into the eyes of the audience, trying to give them a feeling of what I'm feeling. I'm skating for them and for me. When I'm skating well, I can feel them pulling for me. It makes me skate even better."

One key to Reggie's success is that he likes both free skating and the hard work of the sport, the necessary school figures. Most competitors love free skating with its range of whirling and high-flying movements that set an audience on fire. Few skaters enjoy the painstaking demands of school figures.

"I don't know why," Reggie says, "but I don't mind doing the school figures. It's sort of peaceful doing those figure-eight patterns in endless circles. Sure, it can get dull in practice, and it doesn't turn on the crowds. But the judges care about those figures. They make up thirty per cent of your total score."

Looking back over his short, sparkling career, Reggie sees it as a mixture of fun and travel, along with some hard moments. "I was really embarrassed when I skated in France, in 1974. I was right in the middle of my program when I took a flop. Of course, I got up and finished. As I left the ice, the people started yelling, *'Bis! Bis!'* I thought they were laughing at me. Then somebody said that it meant 'Encore!' So I went back and repeated a part of my program. Wouldn't you know it — I fell in the same place as the first time. That was strange, and I felt awful — even though the people clapped.

"But that was only embarrassing, like a bad joke. It was nothing compared to the time when my boot came untied in the middle of my performance. I was moving in perfect time with the music. Then I felt one of my laces loosen, and I started to get scared. I worried, 'Should I do the next jump? I could twist my ankle, maybe break it. Should I stop or take the chance?' Well, I just kept on skating. It's a good thing I did, because nothing happened and I got high marks."

Courage, determination, championship skating — that's Reggie Stanley, who rates top marks for everything he does in life.

The U.S.A.

Quite a country, back and forth,
East and West, and South and North;
Take your pick from sun or snow,
Where the winds of winter blow
Or where softer winds in tune
Turn your winters into June.
You can turn to speeding skis,
You can dip in Southern seas;
You can face the snowbound sweep,
Or where rambler roses creep
You can find a soothing calm
In the shadow of the palm,
Whatsoever sport you wish,
All you do is name your dish.

Grantland Rice

Saturday's Child

by Hilary Beckett

My sister Celine spoke in a soft, sweet voice while I — her little sister Mary Claire (littler by a year, anyway) — tended to stumble over my words. Celine had shining curls. They lay around her shoulders in flowing waves. But I was not as lucky; my hair was straight.

My sister Celine had a complexion as smooth as a doll's skin, whereas I often broke out in pimples. And Celine never, never spilled milk on a clean tablecloth or tripped over her own feet.

So you can imagine that if at times we both happened to be in the same room at the same time, there were often unpleasant comparisons.

"But you are Saturday's child," said my mother. She used to sing me a song I hated about Monday's child being fair of face, and so on, through the entire week to Saturday, the day on which I was born.

Saturday's unfortunate children had only the chance of having to work for a living. It went like this — I couldn't forget it if I tried:

> Monday's child is fair of face,
> Tuesday's child is full of grace,
> Wednesday's child is full of woe,
> Thursday's child has far to go,
> Friday's child is loving and giving,
> Saturday's child works hard for a living,
> But the child who is born on the Sabbath day
> Is blithe and bonny and good — they say.

I never quite knew what "having to work for a living" meant where children were concerned. But I had a strong idea that it was much worse being a Saturday child than being a Sunday child. Sunday's child — Celine, Who else? — was born "blithe and bonny and good . . ." (so the stupid verse went) — *and* lucky!

You'd probably think that I would develop a real grudge against Celine because of her beauty and good looks. No, I was a "good" child. And I believed firmly, as I had been taught, that being a Saturday child affected my life in some strange way beyond my control. So instead of hating Celine, I worked on ways to please her.

Most teachers were surprised to learn that we were sisters. "So you're Celine Dolan's sister! You're not a bit like her at all!" they said.

Throughout the years of my childhood, I believed I could blame all my minor daily disasters on being a Saturday child. If I couldn't play ball, being a Saturday child excused me. Saturday's children easily mislaid lunch boxes, failed to make their beds, or forgot to hang up their clothes. I felt that Saturday's children also made their parents enjoy — all the more — any Sunday child they were lucky to have.

Actually, I began over the years to hide anything good I did from my parents because of my deep feeling that they wouldn't believe me. I really didn't think I was as stupid as I acted. I mean, I *was* kind to small children and animals. And once in a while, I actually gave Celine some help with her homework. But who knew? Or cared?

There was just one thoroughly delightful secret I kept.

I had a secret place in the garage, the garage behind our house. Our house had once been a farmhouse, and the garage had been a barn. The second floor had probably once been used for storing hay. But now this damp, musty area was empty and forgotten.

Here, in this secret hideaway, I played for hours without being disturbed. The first few times I went there, I worried that no one in the house missed me. There were no calls of "Mary Claire! Mary Claa-err!" Then I suspected that I was giving them a welcome rest. Anyway, they knew I'd always return for meals.

One spring day, I took home from school a handful of clay. We had art once a week, and in art period, I'd been delighted by the material. After we had rolled and pounded and punched the clay, Mr. Winsor, the art teacher, had modeled a head for us. Right before our eyes, he'd shaped the clay from a glob into a globe into a skull into a face! He used a friend of mine for his model, and gradually Lucy's eyes appeared under Mr. Winsor's skillful fingers, then her small nose, and then her slightly smiling mouth.

It was a miracle! All the time Mr. Winsor worked so surely, my own hands wanted to try a sculpture of my own. And in the next art period, I did! After that period, I asked Mr. Winsor for some clay, and he told me to help myself and to take some home if I felt like it. When I got home, I took the clay up to my hayloft. I remembered to leave the clay covered with a damp cloth at night — as Mr. Winsor had told us — so that it wouldn't harden before I had finished my sculpture.

At first, I hadn't any idea what I was going to try to make. I mostly enjoyed the squishing and the shaping and the molding of the clay. It felt alive, and I knew that it would direct me to some satisfying project.

Finally, I decided to start on a small model of a girl. The clay seemed to like the idea I had chosen. As I worked, a girl appeared, clasping a bunch of flowers in her arms, close to her body. To make her stand firmly, I modeled some grass around her bare feet. There! With the palms of my hands, with the tips and the flat sides of my own fingers, I'd formed a very satisfying little statue out of a lump of clay.

I let the finished clay figure dry. Each afternoon after school, I ran up the garage steps to admire her standing gracefully there in the afternoon sunlight.

I couldn't figure out what I really wanted to do with her or whether or not I would even permit anyone to see her — until the school's Open House. Even then I didn't make up my mind until I'd thought about it a lot.

This girl was the best thing I had ever made in my fourteen years on this earth. I wasn't at all modest because I knew that she was, without question, an excellent piece of sculpture. I'd been to enough art shows to have a pretty good idea.

I decided to take her to school just on the day of the Open House. This was when all our families visited school one night to see what we had been doing all year in our various classes.

My homeroom teacher praised my work when she saw the little figure. "We absolutely must have Mr. Winsor put it in the kiln after the Open House, Mary Claire, to fire it," she told me. "Dried clay is very fragile if it hasn't been fired."

A card with "Mary Claire Dolan" printed on it was put next to the little figure. My teacher wanted me to call the statue "Spring," but I thought that was corny. Besides, that marvelous little figure was me, or some part of me. I had made her, and she was a little piece of my innermost feelings. It was proof that somewhere in me there was *some* talent and even some beauty.

That night I began to get a headache as my parents and Celine and I inched our way around my classroom at a snail's pace. I felt as if making the little figure with such secrecy had been in some strange way unfair. After all, *they* knew nothing about her! Then I forced my headache away by repeating to myself, "She's mine! I made her!"

My mother — at the head of our group — set eyes on her first.

I caught my breath.

"Oh, how beautiful!" exclaimed my mother. Then, thrilling me with her loving voice (surprised though it was), "Mary Claire, *you* made this? Oh, look at it, Howard! Look, Celine!"

Celine looked, and for a minute, surprise — yes, and envy — flashed across her lovely face. Then she caught herself and turned her eyes from parent to parent, seeing that for once she would have to let me have the center of the stage. "What a terrific surprise, Mary Claire!" she said to me. "What a surprise! Did you mean to make it look like me? Oh, let me see it!"

She grabbed across the table for it, and seemingly by mistake, it slipped out of her hands. The dry clay settled into powdery heaps on the table. My mother gasped with horror.

Celine said, "Oh, I *am* sorry! But it was an accident!"

At first, I was furious with disappointment. But then, because I had memorized every turn, every curve in the little figure, I knew I could make her from memory again whenever I wished. And I knew I could make other beautiful things. In fact, I had a talent that no one, not even Celine, could take from me.

I felt a little sorrowful, too, about Celine. She would never again be the perfect "Sunday child" I had always imagined. She was human, just like me, and I wouldn't let myself be bothered by her anymore. And my parents must have made some mental notes on this, too, for they stopped labeling us.

My mother never called me Saturday's child again. But do you know, I wouldn't have cared anymore!

STOWAWAY!

by **Armando Socarras Ramírez**
as told to **Denis Fodor**
and **John Reddy**

The jet engines thundered as the big plane taxied down the runway at Havana's José Martí Airport. We huddled in the tall grass nearby. For months, my friend Jorge Pérez Blanco and I had been planning to stow away in a wheel well on this flight, No. 904. It was Spain's once-weekly, nonstop run from Havana to Madrid. Now, in the late afternoon of June 3, 1969, our moment had come.

We knew we were pretty young to be taking such a big chance. I was seventeen; Jorge, sixteen. But we were both determined to escape from Cuba, and our plans had been carefully made. We knew that departing airliners taxied to the end of the 11,500-foot runway, stopped

81

briefly after turning around, then roared down the runway to take off. We wore rubber-soled shoes to aid us in crawling up the wheels and carried ropes to tie ourselves inside the wheel well. We had also stuffed cotton in our ears as protection against the noise of the four jet engines. Now we lay sweating with fear as the huge plane swung around, the jet blast flattening the grass all around us. "Let's run!" I shouted to Jorge.

We dashed onto the runway and leaped toward the left wheels of the now stilled plane. As Jorge began to scramble up the forty-two-inch-high tires, I saw there was not room for us both in the single well. "I'll try the other side!" I shouted. Quickly, I climbed onto the right wheels, grabbed a bar and, twisting and wriggling, pulled myself into the semidark well. The plane began rolling immediately, and I grabbed some machinery to keep from falling out. The roar of the engines nearly deafened me.

As we became airborne, the huge double wheels, hot from takeoff, began folding into the compartment. I tried to flatten myself against the overhead wall as they came closer and closer. Then, desperate, I pushed at them with my feet. But they pressed powerfully upward, squeezing me terrifyingly against the roof of the well. Just when I felt that I would be crushed, the wheels locked into place, and the bay doors beneath them closed. So there I was. My five-foot-four-inch, 140-pound frame was wedged in a spaghettilike maze of pipes and machinery. I could not move enough to tie myself to anything, so I stuck my rope behind a pipe.

Then, before I had time to catch my breath, the bay doors suddenly dropped open again, and the wheels stretched out into their landing position. I held on for dear life, wondering if I had been spotted. Could it be that the plane was turning back to hand me over to Castro's police?

By the time the wheels began closing again, I had seen a bit of extra space where I could safely squeeze. Now I knew there *was* room for me, even though I could scarcely breathe. After a few minutes, I touched one of the tires and found that it had cooled off. I swallowed some aspirin tablets for the head-splitting noise and began to wish that I had worn something warmer than my light-weight sport shirt and green pants.

Up in the cockpit of Flight 904, forty-four-year-old Captain Valentín Vara del Rey had settled into the routine of the overnight flight. It would last eight hours and twenty minutes. Takeoff had been normal. But, right after liftoff, something unusual had happened. One of the three red lights on the instrument panel had remained lighted, showing improper closing of the landing gear.

"Are you having difficulty?" the control tower asked.

"Yes," replied Vara del Rey. "There is a signal that the right wheel hasn't closed properly. I'll repeat the procedure."

The captain relowered the landing gear, then raised it again. This time the red light blinked out.

Dismissing the trouble shown by the red light, the captain turned his attention to climbing to the right cruising altitude. On leveling out, he observed that the temperature outside was 41 degrees below zero. Inside, the flight attendants began serving dinner to the 147 passengers.

Shivering from the bitter cold, I wondered if Jorge had made it into the other wheel well. I began thinking about what had brought me to this desperate situation. I thought about my parents and my girl, María Esther, and wondered what they would think when they learned what I had done.

My father is a plumber, and I have four brothers and a sister. We are poor, like most Cubans. Our house in Havana has just one large room; eleven people live in it — or did. Food is scarce, and we could only have a small amount. About the only fun I had was playing baseball and walking with María Esther along the sea wall. When I turned sixteen, the government had shipped me off to school in Betancourt, a village where sugar cane is grown. There I was supposed to learn welding, but classes were often interrupted to send the students off to plant sugar cane.

Young as I was, I was tired of living in a country that controlled everyone's life. I dreamed of freedom. I wanted to become an artist and live in the United States, where I had an uncle. I knew that thousands of Cubans had gone to that nation and done well there. As the time approached when I would be forced to join the army, I thought more and more of trying to get away. But how? I knew that two plane loads of people were allowed to leave Havana for Miami each day. But there was a waiting list of eight hundred thousand for these flights. Also, if you signed up to leave, the government looked on you as a *gusano* — a worm — and life would become even less bearable.

It seemed hopeless. Then I met Jorge at a Havana baseball game. After the game, we started talking. I found out that Jorge and I had the same feelings about Cuba. "The system takes away your freedom — forever," he complained.

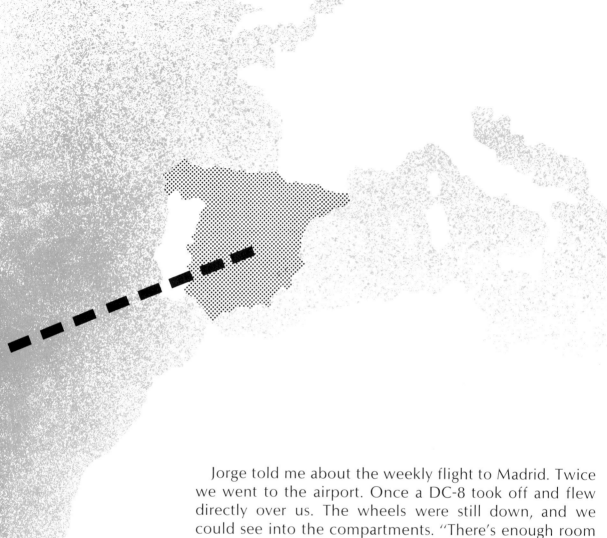

Jorge told me about the weekly flight to Madrid. Twice we went to the airport. Once a DC-8 took off and flew directly over us. The wheels were still down, and we could see into the compartments. "There's enough room in there for me," I remembered saying.

These were my thoughts as I lay in the freezing darkness more than five miles above the Atlantic Ocean. By now we had been in the air about an hour, and I was getting lightheaded from the lack of oxygen. Was it really only a few hours earlier that I had bicycled through the rain with Jorge and hidden in the grass? Was Jorge safe? My parents? María Esther? Then I blacked out.

The sun rose over the Atlantic as the DC-8 crossed the European coast high over Portugal. With the end of the 5563-mile flight in sight, Captain Vara del Rey began his descent toward Madrid's Barajas Airport. Arrival would be at 8:00 A.M. local time. The weather in Madrid was sunny and pleasant.

Vara del Rey started to let down his landing gear. A two-hundred-miles-per-hour wind force swirled through the wheel wells. The plane went into its final approach. Then flame and smoke spurted from the tires as the DC-8 touched down at about one hundred forty miles per hour.

It was a perfect landing — no bumps. After a brief post-flight check, Vara del Rey walked down the steps and stood by the nose of the plane, waiting for a car to pick up him and his crew.

Nearby, there was a sudden soft plop as my frozen body fell to the ground beneath the plane. José Rocha Lorenzana, a security guard, was the first to reach my crumpled figure. "When I touched his clothes, they were as stiff as wood," José Rocha Lorenzana said. "All he did was make a strange sound, a kind of moan."

"I couldn't believe it at first," Vara del Rey said when told about me. "But then I went over to see him. He had ice over his nose and mouth. And his color . . . " As he watched my unconscious body being bundled into a truck, the captain kept exclaiming to himself, "Impossible! Impossible!"

The first thing I remember after losing consciousness was hitting the ground at the Madrid airport. Then I blacked out again and woke up later at a hospital in downtown Madrid. I was more dead than alive. When they took my temperature, it was so low that it did not even register on the thermometer. "Am I in Spain?" was my first question. And then, "Where's Jorge?" (Jorge is believed to have been knocked down by the jet blast while trying to climb into the other wheel well and to be in prison in Cuba.)

Doctors said later that my condition was like that of a patient undergoing "deep freeze" surgery — a delicate process performed only under carefully controlled conditions. Dr. José María Pajares, who cared for me, called my survival a "medical miracle." I feel lucky to be alive.

A few days after my escape, I was up and around the hospital. I played cards with my police guard and read stacks of letters from all over the world. I especially liked one from a girl in California. "You are a hero," she wrote, "but not very wise." My uncle, Elo Fernández, who lives in New Jersey, telephoned and invited me to come to the United States to live with him. The International Rescue Committee arranged my passage and has continued to help me.

I am fine now. I live with my uncle and go to school to learn English. I still hope to study to be an artist.

I often think of my friend Jorge. We both knew the risk we were taking and the fact that we might be killed in our attempt to escape from Cuba. But it seemed worth the chance.

One Chance in a Million

Charles Glasgow, a vice president of the Douglas Aircraft Company, which makes the DC-8, says that there is "one chance in a million" that a person would not be crushed when the huge double wheels of the plane are raised. "There is space for a person in there," he says, "but that person would have to be a contortionist to fit in between the wheels."

He also says that Armando should have died from both the lack of oxygen and the extreme cold. Since the cruising altitude of Flight 904 was twenty-nine thousand feet, the oxygen content of the air was about half that at sea level. The temperature was 41 degrees below zero. At that altitude, in an unpressurized, unwarmed compartment, a person would normally be conscious for only two or three minutes and live only a short while longer.

Perhaps a Spanish doctor best summed up Armando's experience by saying, "He survived with luck, luck, luck — many tons of luck."

Survival Skill

Reading a Newspaper

How do you read a newspaper? Do you start on page one and read all the way through? Or do you find your favorite part and read that part first? If you are looking for a certain part of the newspaper, the index can help you. It lists in alphabetical order the parts and features that appear in the newspaper. The index is printed on the first or second page of most newspapers.

Below is the index to the *Swansea Journal*. The index to most newspapers looks something like this one.

SWANSEA JOURNAL

Index

Read the list of entries. This index gives only the first page of each part and feature. It does not list all the pages included in each part. Did you notice that NEWS is not listed? Why do you think it is not listed? Of course, you would find news stories in many parts of the newspaper.

Now read the first entry. That part has news about works of art and about films. The stories on those pages cover such subjects as music, dance, plays, paintings, sculpture, photography, and movies. It also gives the times that museums are open and the types of exhibits that are held there. If you wanted to find out the times for a movie at a local theater, would you look in the ARTS/ FILMS part? Yes, that part gives the movie schedule. Movie and play reviews usually tell something about the plot of each and list the important actors. They also tell what the reviewer liked or did not like about them.

The CLASSIFIED pages have all kinds of ads. Those ads are not like the display ads for department stores and for different kinds of products. The classified ads are printed in small type, take little space, and are grouped together by subject. For instance, all the ads for pets may be under the heading "Dogs, Cats, Pets." Most newspapers have headings for real estate, apartments for rent, legal notices, machinery and tools, auctions, lost and found, personals, and automobiles. Your newspaper may have more or fewer headings than the ones given here. If you wanted to find an apartment to rent, would you look in the CLASSIFIED part of the paper? Yes, you would look under the heading "Apartments for Rent."

Two regular features in many newspapers are the comics and the crossword puzzle. On the comics page, you can follow the adventures of your favorite cartoon characters. Many people enjoy completing a crossword puzzle in their spare time.

DEATH NOTICES are sometimes listed as OBITUARIES. That part of the paper gives facts about people who have died recently. The people listed are usually those who lived in the area, but many times death notices about well-known people are included too. You would look there if you wanted to find out the time and place of a funeral for a certain person.

The newspaper prints opinions of news events and issues in the EDITORIALS part. The articles appearing there are called editorials. Because they are usually opinions, they differ from many of the news stories that are based on facts. Usually included in the EDITORIALS part are letters to the editor. These are letters that are sent to the newspaper by its readers. The letters are about news issues or editorials that were printed in an earlier edition of the newspaper. Look again at the index. Do you see LETTERS? You can see that the page number for EDITORIALS and LETTERS is the same.

What information, do you think, would be given under FAMILY LIVING? News about life styles, fashion, personal and medical advice, and food are given in that part. Coupons and supermarket ads usually appear there. Would you look in FAMILY LIVING to find out the best food bargains this week? Yes, you would find that kind of information there.

News about business, money, credit, and the stock market are printed in the FINANCE part of the paper.

The SPORTS part gives current news about all the major sports events. On those pages, you might find interviews with well-known sports figures. A list of sports events for that day or week might be printed there too. Do you think that an article about the kinds of boats used for fishing would appear in the SPORTS part? Yes, it would. That part also gives news about nonteam sports.

The TELEVISION/RADIO part is printed daily in most newspapers. The TV guide is similar to the one you learned about on pages 26–27. Sometimes there are also news stories about television actors and reviews of television shows. Included in that part are a list of radio stations and a schedule of the radio programs. Usually there is a guide that tells you the numbers on the radio dial where each station is. Let's say that you wanted to spend an hour listening to country and western music. You would read to find which radio station has a program of this kind and where on the radio dial that station is located.

A regular feature printed in most newspapers is the weather report. On the page where the weather report is, you can find your area's expected high and low temperatures for the day as well as yesterday's high and low temperatures. Weather conditions for the major regions of the nation are also usually given. The times for the rising of the sun and moon and the setting of each are often listed. If you wanted to find out the number of hours of daylight for today, would you look there? Yes, this kind of information appears on that page.

You can see that the newspaper index helps you find quickly the part of the paper you want to read. So, the next time you want to find your favorite part or feature, use the index.

Now use the *Swansea Journal* index on page 88 to answer the following items. Use a separate piece of paper. Write the number of each item and the letter of the correct answer.

1. Jeff wants to see a play at a theater in Swansea. In which part of the newspaper would he find a list of the plays being performed?
    a. SPORTS   c. ARTS/FILMS
    b. TELEVISION/RADIO   d. CLASSIFIED

2. Michelle wrote a letter to the newspaper about the tax increase. To which page in the newspaper should she turn to find out if her letter was printed?
    a. 41   c. 17
    b. 22   d. 30

3. Nicky and Rex wonder which items are on sale at the supermarket. Which part of the newspaper might help them decide what to buy this week?
    a. FAMILY LIVING   c. FINANCE
    b. CLASSIFIED   d. EDITORIALS

4. Ms. Michaels lost her watch while she was downtown. Which part of the newspaper should she read to see if her watch has been found?
    a. DEATH NOTICES   c. COMICS
    b. CLASSIFIED   d. FAMILY LIVING

5. Ron wants to find out if the Blades hockey team is playing at the Civic Center tonight. To find out, he should turn to page
    a. 19.   c. 17.
    b. 30.   d. 25.

THE CASE OF THE PUNJABI RUBY

by Frank Willment

CHARACTERS

Madame Martine, *jewelry-shop owner*
Mona La Marr, *movie actress*
Silas Small, *financier*
Sardu Singh, *representative of a rajah*
Bradford Cabot, *museum curator*
Sergeant O'Shea, *police officer*
Officer Akimoto, *police officer*
Inspector Conlon, *police officer*
Miss Agatha Pritchett, *retired schoolteacher*

Time: Late afternoon

Setting: A small room in the rear of Madame Martine's jewelry shop. At center stage is a long table with five chairs around it. There are a few chairs, an end table, and other pieces of furniture around the room. There is a telephone on a table upstage. Doors are at the right and at the left.

At Rise: Sergeant O'Shea stands at center stage in front of the table, talking to Mona La Marr, who is seated at one end of the table. Bradford Cabot stands behind her, listening. Madame Martine is seated at the opposite end of the table, going through the contents of her pocketbook. Sardu Singh is pacing back and forth at the rear of the room. Silas Small sits at the left, lost in thought, and Officer Akimoto is guarding the door at the right.

Mona La Marr: *(angrily and excitedly)* Why are you keeping us here, Sergeant? We've all been thoroughly searched by you or the officer. *(She waves a hand in the direction of Officer Akimoto.)* None of us has the missing ruby!

O'Shea: A few minutes more, Miss La Marr. Inspector Conlon should be here any second. I called him at home as soon as the robbery was reported. It isn't every day that we have a half-million-dollar jewel stolen in this city.

Singh: *(angrily)* It was more than just a jewel. It was the Punjabi Ruby, a national treasure of my country, taken from us years ago.

Small: *(rising and crossing to the center)* You say it was the Punjabi Ruby, Singh. All we know is that we were looking at a very valuable stone. The lights went out and it was gone. *(to O'Shea)* What can Inspector Conlon do, Sergeant, that you and the officer haven't already done? You've searched us; you've searched the room. The gem isn't here. Let us go home while you continue your investigation.

O'Shea: My orders are not to let anyone leave, Mr. Small. You'll all be free to go shortly, I'm sure. *(A knock on the door is heard.)* There's the inspector now. Let him in, Akimoto.

Akimoto: Right, Sergeant. *(She opens the door at the right, and Inspector Conlon and Miss Agatha Pritchett enter.)*

Conlon: *(moves to sit on edge of table as others gather around him)* Sorry to inconvenience you folks, but we'll have a better chance of solving this mess if we keep you all together. This is Miss Agatha Pritchett. *(He indicates Agatha, who nods and smiles.)* She taught me a few things years ago when she was my seventh-grade teacher. She happened to be paying me a visit when the sergeant's telephone call came. She asked to tag along to see a police investigation of a robbery firsthand.

O'Shea: You picked a good one, Miss Pritchett. This case is a real humdinger.

Miss Agatha: Please call me Miss Agatha. Everyone does. Now, all of you pretend that I'm not here.

Conlon: I'm sure nobody minds, Miss Agatha. Now, then, let's get down to work. Will you fill us in on the facts, O'Shea?

O'Shea: Sure, Inspector. *(indicating Martine)* This is Madame Martine, the owner of this shop, Martine's Jewels. *(Conlon nods.)* You passed through the main shop to get to this room. This is where she conducts private auctions of rare jewels.

Conlon: And I gather that an auction was going on here this afternoon.

Martine: Yes, we were holding a

small quiet auction of a valuable ruby. I had invited four clients who had expressed an interest in purchasing the gem.

Conlon: All four clients are present, I presume?

Martine: Yes, Inspector. *(She indicates La Marr.)* This is Mona La Marr, the actress. *(She indicates Singh.)* This gentleman is Sardu Singh. The rajah he represents is an old client of mine. *(She indicates Bradford Cabot.)* Bradford Cabot is the curator of the City Museum.

Agatha: Pardon me for interrupting. Mr. Cabot, most curators have a specialty. Do you, sir?

Cabot: Yes, Madam. I am in charge of our collection of minerals, metals, fossils, and gems.

Martine: There is one more client you have not met, Inspector. *(She indicates Small.)* This is Silas Small, a well-known financier.

Small: I trust this won't take too long, Inspector. I'd like to get back to the stock exchange before closing time.

Conlon: I understand. Tell me, Mr. Small, were you representing some business organization at the auction this afternoon?

Small: No, I'm strictly a private collector. As a matter of fact, I would appreciate as little publicity as possible. The fewer people who know I collect rare

gems, the less chance I have of being robbed.

Conlon: Now, let's see if I have the facts straight. Miss Martine was conducting a private auction in this room this afternoon, with four clients bidding on a valuable ruby.

Martine: We were sitting around this table with the ruby on a black cloth in the center.

Conlon: You, Miss Martine, were sitting at the head, I suppose?

Martine: Yes. Miss La Marr and Mr. Small were on my right, and Mr. Cabot was on my left.

Conlon: Then at the far end of the table was Mr. Singh, the representative of the rajah of something-or-other.

Singh: *(angrily)* If you please! There was a time in my country when such rudeness would have cost you your head!

Conlon: Fortunately for me, those days are gone, and we aren't in your country. Now, Miss Martine, tell us about your ruby.

Martine: It wasn't mine, Inspector. I was only trying to sell it for another client. I was working on a commission basis.

Conlon: How much commission would you have received?

Martine: Twenty per cent. That's the standard fee in jewel auctions.

Agatha: Then if the gem had been auctioned for half a million dollars, your commission would have been $100,000.

Martine: Quite true. However, with the ruby gone, I receive nothing. You can see why I am anxious for its return.

Conlon: Who is the owner of the ruby, Miss Martine?

Martine: A wealthy European man who wishes to remain unknown.

Conlon: There's no doubt that the ruby was real?

Cabot: No doubt at all. I inspected it carefully, using a jeweler's loupe. In all modesty, I must say that I am an expert with jewels.

Small: I consider myself something of an expert also. I examined the gem, and I can say with certainty that it was genuine.

Singh: I may not be an expert, but I would know the Punjabi Ruby anywhere. The gem on the table an hour ago *was* the Punjabi Ruby!

Conlon: I'll accept the fact that it was genuine. Now, what actually happened at the auction?

Martine: We met here at one P.M., examined the ruby, placed it in the center of the table, and began the bidding.

La Marr: We hadn't been bidding too long before there was a power failure. The lights went out, and since there are no windows in the room, it was completely dark.

Conlon: How long were the lights out?

La Marr: Perhaps ten or fifteen seconds, Inspector. Not very long.

Singh: But quite long enough! When the lights went on again, the Punjabi Ruby was missing!

Conlon: Could anyone have entered the room while the lights were out?

Martine: Impossible. There are two doors, and both were locked. And, of course, the room has no windows.

Conlon: Could anyone have hidden in the room before the auction began?

O'Shea: Impossible, Inspector.

There's no place to hide. There isn't even a closet in the room.

Conlon: Then that brings us back to the five people at the table when the lights went out. Now, what happened when the lights went on?

Small: We discovered immediately that the ruby was missing.

Cabot: I insisted that the police be called at once and that no one leave the room.

Agatha: There is a telephone in the room, I presume?

Martine: Yes, over on the corner table. I did not leave the room to make a phone call, if that is what you're suggesting, Miss Aggie.

Conlon: How long did it take Sergeant O'Shea and Officer Akimoto to arrive?

La Marr: Less than five minutes, I would say.

Akimoto: That's about right, Inspector. The station house is only two blocks away. We left as soon as we got the message.

Conlon: What did you do when you got here, Sergeant O'Shea?

O'Shea: Akimoto and I searched the shop thoroughly after we questioned the witnesses.

Conlon: Did you turn up anything in your search, O'Shea?

O'Shea: Not a single clue and, of course, no sign of the ruby.

Akimoto: After that, we decided to search the people who were present when the robbery took place.

O'Shea: Akimoto searched the two women; I searched the three men.

Cabot: *(earnestly)* We insisted on a thorough search.

La Marr: It was obvious that the ruby must still be in the room, so each of us insisted on clearing herself or himself.

Conlon: I gather the personal search also proved fruitless.

O'Shea: That's right. None of them had the ruby.

Conlon: Did anyone leave the room — even for a moment, perhaps?

La Marr: No one left the room at any time. We were watching each other like hawks!

Conlon: It looks as if we have the elements of a first-rate mystery on our hands, doesn't it?

O'Shea: I'll say! We made a complete list of everything found on the suspects during the search.

La Marr: Suspects! I've never been so insulted in my life.

Agatha: *(gently)* But, Miss La Marr, one of you has to be guilty. So all of you are suspects.

La Marr: You're right, I suppose. It just doesn't sound very nice.

Conlon: O'Shea, do you have the lists made of the suspects' possessions?

O'Shea: *(taking note pad from his pocket and giving it to Conlon)* Here they are, Inspector. There was nothing of any importance on anyone.

Conlon: *(glancing at the lists)* So I see. Combs, keys, handkerchiefs, wallets — there is nothing out of the ordinary.

Agatha: *(timidly, to Conlon)* May I see the lists, Bill?

Conlon: Well, I don't know. You're not on the force, Miss Agatha.

Small: Why do you want to poke your nose into our affairs?

Agatha: You seem to have reached a dead end. I thought that something on the lists might be helpful — give the inspector another lead, you know.

La Marr: I certainly have nothing to hide.

Cabot: Read them aloud. Somebody may get an idea. I'm sure we all want to find the ruby and go home.

Conlon: No objections? *(He looks around at the group.)* All right, read the lists out loud, Miss Agatha. *(He gives her the lists.)*

Agatha: Let's see. The first list is Mr. Small's. *(reading)* "Handkerchief, aspirin, jeweler's loupe, checkbook, wallet, change." Here's Mona La Marr's list. *(reading)* "Compact, lipstick, doctor's prescription, credit cards, money clip, address book, sunglasses, mints, keys, change purse, tissues." Now this is Mr. Singh's list. *(reading)* "Passport, beads, letter of introduction, traveler's checks, wallet, eye drops, cold tablets." Now here is

Madame Martine's list. *(reading)* "Perfume, compact, lipstick, chewing gum, datebook, tissues, keys, pocket calculator, brush, comb."

Singh: The pocket calculator was to figure her twenty per cent commission on the Punjabi Ruby!

Martine: A legal commission!

Agatha: Here's the last list — Mr. Cabot's. *(reading)* "Pipe, tobacco, handkerchief, wallet, credit cards, nail file, parking ticket, comb, keys, jeweler's loupe."

Agatha: Now I've read all the lists.

La Marr: And they weren't much help, were they?

Agatha: Oh, I wouldn't say that. They were most interesting.

Conlon: If you saw something we didn't see, tell us, Miss Agatha.

Agatha: *(smiling modestly)* To be frank, I did notice one or two little things, but they're probably unimportant.

Akimoto: Then where do we go from here, Inspector?

Conlon: Let's review the facts. Fact one: The ruby must still be in this room. Fact two: It hasn't been found in the room or on anyone who was in the room when it disappeared. This is an interesting case!

Agatha: Let's see what the loss of the ruby would mean to everyone. Perhaps this will show us who had a reason for the theft. That jewel might have been more important to one person than to another. Now, Miss Martine, if the gem had been sold for $500,000, your commission would have been $100,000. Is that correct?

Martine: Yes, the theft cost me $100,000. How is that for a motive?

Agatha: Wasn't the ruby insured?

Martine: Of course, it was insured for its full value by the owner in Europe. He will collect the insurance.

Agatha: I see. The owner loses nothing. But you lose your commission.

Martine: That is correct.

Agatha: Actually, the others have lost nothing except the chance to bid on the gem. Perhaps it would be enlightening to see what each person at the auction intended to do with the ruby and how much each was prepared to pay.

Conlon: That's a good angle to pursue, Miss Agatha.

Agatha: Let's start with you, Miss La Marr. Why did you want the stone?

La Marr: Frankly, wearing beautiful jewels is part of my image. Gossip columns often mention my jewels. The ruby would be worth tons of publicity to me. It would have given my career a big boost.

Agatha: I quite understand. And how much were you willing to pay?

La Marr: Unfortunately, this auction caught me at a bad time. I could only raise $275,000.

Agatha: I see. And how high had the bidding gone when the lights went out?

Martine: The bidding was at $130,000. And the auction was far from over.

Agatha: Mr. Cabot, you said you wanted to purchase the ruby for your museum. How high were you allowed to go, may I ask?

Cabot: I suppose there's no harm in telling you now. My top figure was to be $350,000. But I hoped to get it for less.

Agatha: If you had been the successful bidder, the gem would be put on display at the museum?

Cabot: Correct.

Agatha: Mr. Small, if you, however, had bought the ruby, it would have been hidden from the world.

Small: As a private collector, I have no wish to share my treasures with people. Gems are my hobby.

Agatha: I see. And how much were you prepared to spend on your hobby?

Small: The auction was called at a bad time for me, to tell you the truth. Usually, I would not have permitted anyone to outbid me, but I lost a lot of money on the stock market last week. A bid of $225,000 would have been my top offer today.

Agatha: Then you, like Miss La Marr, would have lost to Mr. Cabot and the City Museum.

Small: It would seem so.

Singh: Not quite! You seem to have forgotten that I was also bidding on the stone!

Agatha: I was coming to you, Mr. Singh. What did you intend to do with the ruby?

Singh: It was the Punjabi Ruby! I was to return it to my homeland and to my rajah, the rightful owner! Eighteen years ago, it was stolen from the Shrine of Jind.

Agatha: Then it would have been displayed in the shrine?

Singh: Yes. My instructions were to outbid everyone, and the rajah is wealthy enough to do just that!

Agatha: According to the others, the top bid would have been Mr. Cabot's $350,000.

Singh: Then I would have secured the ruby for $360,000.

Agatha: I see. I thank all of you for your frank answers, but I haven't been too much help so far, I'm afraid.

Conlon: Oh, one can't have too much information in a case like this. One slip of the tongue could provide the key to the mystery.

(All talk with each other.)

Agatha: *(leading Conlon aside, whispering)* My thoughts exactly, Bill — one slip of the tongue.

Conlon: Then we'll have to watch for it.

Agatha: Oh, it's already happened.

Conlon: It has? Do you know where the ruby is and who stole it?

Agatha: I think so, but I'm not certain of my facts yet. May I make one more suggestion?

Conlon: Of course. You seem to have missed your career, Miss Agatha. You would have made quite a detective. What do you suggest?

Agatha: *(turning to the others, brightly)* I think it would be interesting to re-enact the crime. Everybody could sit around the table. We could go through the bidding, then turn out the lights at the proper moment, turn them on after ten seconds or so, and see if we learn anything.

Cabot: It sounds silly. What could we possibly learn?

Agatha: Perhaps where the jewel is and who took it.

Conlon: What can we lose? The ruby is gone. Let's try it. Take the places you had at the time of

100

the auction. *(They take their seats around the table, with Martine at head, Singh at the opposite end, La Marr and Small to the right of Martine, Cabot to her left.)* Now, let's put the black cloth in the center — without the Punjabi Ruby, of course. *(Martine unfolds the cloth and lays it on the table.)*

Conlon: Please conduct the auction, Miss Martine. Sergeant O'Shea, go over by the light switch. *(Conlon motions to the left.)* When the bidding reaches

$130,000, as it did earlier today, turn off the lights for ten seconds, and then switch them back on.

O'Shea: *(going left to light switch)* Will do, Inspector.

Conlon: Go ahead, Miss Martine.

(Conlon stations himself behind the table; Miss Agatha stands at the head of the table behind Martine; Akimoto is at the other end of the table behind Sardu Singh.)

Martine: Very well. You have all examined the ruby. May we begin the bidding?

Small: I bid $50,000.

La Marr: Make that $60,000.

Cabot: I say $70,000.

Singh: Let's stop these small bids. I'll bid $100,000.

Small: Make it $110,000.

La Marr: $120,000.

Cabot: It's $130,000 here.

(O'Shea flips the light switch, and there is a blackout for ten seconds. The lights come up again. A large ruby is in the center of the table on the black cloth.)

Singh: *(surprised)* Look! The ruby is back in place! Praise be!

Conlon: Jumping catfish! It is back!

Akimoto: Is it the real Punjabi Ruby?

Cabot: *(taking out jeweler's loupe and examining gem)* It's the real thing, all right.

Small: Let me see it! *(He takes the ruby from Cabot, takes out his*

loupe and examines it.) He's right! It is the Punjabi Ruby!

Martine: It has been found! How wonderful! Now we can continue the auction.

Singh: No auction is necessary. Miss Agatha had us show our top bids. I am the highest bidder at $360,000. Can anyone top it?

Conlon: You can't bid on stolen property, Mr. Singh. A crime is involved.

Martine: But the ruby is back, even if we don't know who returned it!

Agatha: I know who returned it.

La Marr: You do?

Agatha: Yes. I returned it.

Cabot: You? But you couldn't have. You weren't even here when the gem was stolen!

Agatha: Oh, I didn't steal the ruby. I simply discovered who did, guessed where it was hidden, and returned it to the table while the lights were out.

O'Shea: Well, don't keep us in suspense! Who did it?

Agatha: Let me first explain how I came to my conclusions. Miss La Marr wouldn't steal the ruby. She wanted publicity, and she couldn't wear a stolen gem in public.

Conlon: And Mr. Cabot couldn't have displayed a stolen gem in his museum.

Agatha: Correct. Mr. Singh wanted to return the ruby to his native land. Since he claims it was originally stolen from a shrine, he might have been willing to steal it back. But, if Mr. Singh had stolen the gem, how would he have gotten it out of the country? Both the police and the customs officials would have been watching him like hawks.

La Marr: Then it must have been Silas Small!

Agatha: Mr. Small seemed obvious in the beginning. Once the ruby was in his private collection, no one would know he possessed it. On the other hand, anyone of you might have stolen it, hoping to sell it later to some other private collector who wouldn't question where it came from.

Akimoto: Then we're right back where we were, Miss Agatha.

Agatha: Not quite. While anyone might have had a reason for stealing the ruby, everyone except the thief lacked one important thing.

Akimoto: What was that?

Agatha: Opportunity!

O'Shea: But everyone at the table had the same opportunity. They were all there when the lights went out.

Agatha: But only one person knew *when* the lights would go out.

Akimoto: Who did?

Agatha: The thief. *(to Conlon)* Do you remember that I stopped to chat with the guard when we entered the building?

Conlon: Oh, yes. What did you say to him?

Agatha: Sergeant O'Shea had mentioned the power failure when he talked to you on the telephone. I asked the guard about it.

Conlon: And what did he say?

Agatha: He wasn't aware of a power failure.

Martine: It lasted only ten seconds. He might not have noticed it.

Agatha: I thought that too. So as we walked through the lobby, I spoke to a woman who was leaving the building. I asked her if the blackout had bothered her. She wasn't aware that there had been a power failure either.

Akimoto: Then what caused the lights to go out during the auction?

Agatha: I wondered about that too. I looked around rather carefully when I first arrived. You have rather fancy lighting, don't you, Miss Martine?

Martine: Yes, to show off jewels to their advantage. It's one of the tricks of the trade.

Agatha: At home, I have a timing device attached to my radio. It allows me to go to sleep to the sound of music and to awaken to it. It turns off my radio at night and turns it back on in the morning.

Conlon: Do you mean that by using a timing device, the thief could know exactly when the lights would go off and come on?

Agatha: It occurred to me that it could explain why the lights went out in this room and nowhere else.

Conlon: Miss Martine, do you own such timing devices?

Martine: *(angrily)* What if I do? If that's what caused the lights to go out, anyone of us could have set the timers!

Agatha: I suppose that's true, but first let me explain how I found the ruby.

Akimoto: Please do. I can't wait!

Agatha: It all started when Miss Martine called me Miss Aggie.

Martine: I did?

Agatha: Yes. It was then that I believed you must have been a student of mine at one time.

Martine: But the inspector — you said that he had been a student of yours — and he's been calling you Miss Aggie.

Agatha: No, he's been calling me Miss Agatha. As a matter of fact, I asked everyone to call me Miss Agatha.

Martine: So what?

Agatha: In class, students always called me Miss Agatha. Behind my back, some students called me Miss Aggie, and you were one of them, Molly.

Martine: Molly! What are you talking about?

Agatha: When you said "Miss Aggie," it started to come back.

"Martine," I said to myself, "Martine. Take off the *e*, and you have Martin. Molly Martin, a freckle-faced, gum-chewing, pony-tailed seventh grader!"

Martine: I don't know what you're talking about.

Agatha: *(ignoring her)* That's what I was looking for when I went over the lists. If you were Molly Martin, you'd still chew gum; I was certain. Sure enough, chewing gum was one of the things on your list.

Martine: All right. I used to be in your class, and I still chew gum. How does that add up to a jewel theft?

Agatha: *(to Conlon)* Bill, did you chew gum in school?

Conlon: *(trying to remember)* Yes, I guess I did.

Agatha: Did you chew it in my class, Bill?

Conlon: In your class? Of course not! You had no mercy for gum chewers.

Agatha: Then what did you do with your gum when you were in my classroom?

Conlon: *(thinking a moment)* Why, we all stuck it under our chairs.

Agatha: I thought you would remember that. And I thought that Molly Martin would too! When the sergeant turned off the lights, I reached under her chair and found what I expected to find — a wad of chewing gum.

Conlon: With the Punjabi Ruby in the middle!

Agatha: Correct! I pulled the ruby out of the gum and put it back on the table before the lights came on again!

Conlon: The ruby was under Miss Martine's chair! She was the only one who could really have arranged for the lights to go out. She must have planned the whole thing!

Martine: You're crazy! Why would I steal the gem? I'd lose the huge commission that I'd make on the sale of the ruby.

Agatha: Yes, you'd lose the commission, but you would have the ruby. At another time, when the stock market was better, Mr. Small would have paid you the gem's full worth — $500,000.

Small: I would have, and Miss Martine, or whatever her name is, knows it.

Martine: All right, so I hid the ruby under the chair. What's the charge?

Conlon: It seems to me that you were trying to steal the ruby from its rightful owner. We'll hold you for questioning and get in touch with the owner to see if he wishes to press charges. In any case, I'm pretty sure he won't want you to handle any more auctions for him.

(Akimoto and O'Shea escort Martine out.)

Agatha: *(shaking her head)* Molly Martin was never able to get away with anything, not even back in the seventh grade.

Conlon: Miss Agatha, you should have been a detective.

Agatha: No, Bill, I'll let you be the detective. I'm just a retired schoolteacher. All I did was use one of the tricks of my trade.

LIGHT MY FIRE

by Richard B. Lyttle

The scene was Tiger Stadium in Detroit; the occasion, another World Series. But this time, it was not the game that made history. It was the way the game was introduced. The national anthem, sung before the start of the fifth game of the 1968 World Series, was different from the way it had ever sounded before.

José Feliciano strummed his guitar while he sang a soul version of "The Star-Spangled Banner" in a high tenor voice with feeling and spirit — the way he thought it should be sung.

When the national anthem was over, some in the crowd were too stunned to applaud. Some even thought the way it was sung was unpatriotic. Long after the ball game, long after the baseball season ended for the year, the talk about the Feliciano handling of the national anthem kept on. Everyone wanted to know who José Feliciano was.

People soon learned that José Feliciano was someone special in the world of modern music. In five and a half years as a professional, the young Puerto Rican had climbed from poverty to success. The story of José Feliciano is more than one from rags to riches. It is a story of great determination and courage, for José was born blind.

José was the second of eight sons born to the Feliciano family in a poor farming district of Puerto Rico. When José was five, his father quit trying to earn a living from the soil, and the family moved to New York City to the area known as Spanish Harlem.

The Felicianos remained poor, but the children were always laughing and having fun. José, blind and over-protected by his parents, was cut off from much of the fun — the ball games and other play. He had to learn to amuse himself.

Very early in life, the radio and its music became important to him. José learned how to play the concertina and the guitar. Popular singers became José's heroes. He believed that as a singer, he could earn a living. He was determined not to let his blindness stand in the way of a career in music.

José could not read music, but he had a natural talent for learning music by ear. This talent and hard work began to bring him recognition. Not quite ten years old, José gave his first public appearance at El Teatro Puerto Rico in New York City.

Later, at Charles Evans Hughes High School, José was in demand for school assemblies. He was an expert at copying the styles and voices of famous singers, which delighted his fellow students. These school assemblies gave José a chance to test audience reaction. But he knew that to build his career, he would have to start being paid for singing.

Carrying his guitar in a large paper bag, José began to visit the coffee houses in Greenwich Village, an area in New York City. After entering a coffee house, José would ask the manager for permission to play a few songs. Most managers said they did not have time to listen. José would shrug and ask if he could at least tune his guitar before leaving. Even the busiest manager could not refuse that request. Of course, the guitar would already be tuned. As soon as José pulled it from the paper bag, he would play with such zest that both the manager and customers were delighted.

The customers wanted to hear more of José's music, and they were willing to pay for it. José was on his way to becoming a professional singer.

While playing in a coffee house, José met Hilda Perez, a premedical student. She encouraged José to seek a career in music.

José was seventeen when he accepted his first professional job at a Detroit nightclub. Then later that year, he returned to New York to play at Gerde's Folk City. Commenting on José's performance there, Robert Shelton in the July 13, 1963, issue of *The New York Times* called José a "ten-fingered wizard who romps, runs, rolls, and picks . . . his six strings" in a way no one can match. Shelton recommended Feliciano to those who wanted to see the birth of a star. This review brought the singer more public attention, and nightclub bookings began stacking up.

While still at Gerde's, José met a representative of RCA Victor recording company. Soon after this meeting, José signed an exclusive contract with RCA.

In the fall of 1963, José was performing at a nightclub in Miami, Florida, and there José and Hilda decided to get married. José's marriage made him want to work harder than ever. He appeared on national television for the first time as a guest on the "Al Hirt Show," and RCA released his first album, *The Voice and Guitar of José Feliciano.*

Most reviews of the album were good, but one critic said that José's original guitar style overshadowed his singing. His voice was not outstanding. It sounded too much like other singers. José remembered that in his high-school performances, he had followed the styles and sounds of other singers. He realized that by doing

this, he had slowed the development of a style that was all his own.

About six months after the release of his first album, RCA came out with José's second album, *Bag Full of Soul*. Although it drew much praise, José did not feel right about making records. He was more at ease with a live audience. With an audience, he could judge the response as he went along. José also realized that part of

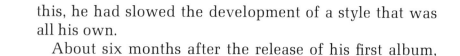

the trouble in recording was that his New York manager wanted José's style to alternate from rock to country music, even when it did not fit his mood or desire.

Wanting to develop his own singing style, he and Hilda decided to move from New York to California. In California, José signed with new managers who agreed to put off recording until he felt ready.

In the meantime, José went on a tour in Latin America. There he sang his songs in Spanish. He was a great success, but better still, the songs in his native tongue proved to be just what he needed to build a style of his own.

RCA International recorded three Spanish albums from José's tours. The records sold well, and two songs, "La Copa Rota" and "Amor Gitana," climbed close to the top of the Latin American popularity charts.

After his tour, José played for Spanish-speaking audiences in the United States. Then he agreed to a television show to be shown on Spanish-language stations in the United States.

By the spring of 1968, José was ready to try another English-language album. This, his third by RCA Victor, was called *Feliciano!* It was his best, and one song in the album carried José to national fame. That song was "Light My Fire," a tune first sung by The Doors, a rock group. José changed it to a soul song, slow and rhythmic. He never expected it to become a big hit. But a hit it was! "Light My Fire" sounded from radios and juke boxes across the land.

Pictures of and stories about José Feliciano appeared in national magazines. He played before sell-out crowds in cities and towns throughout the United States. Everywhere he went, audiences were impressed by his talent, unusual style, and humor.

It was no surprise when he was invited to sing the national anthem to open the fifth game of the 1968 World Series. The surprise came when he raised his head and sang. Millions of people heard José's soul version of "The Star-Spangled Banner." He changed the melody and the meter and filled the song with new meaning.

José's performance at the World Series sparked his career. In April 1969, he starred in his own television special. Then the next month, the National Academy of Recording Arts and Sciences made its awards for the best musical recordings for the year 1968. José received two awards, called Grammies. One was for the best new musical artist, and the other was for the best male popular singer.

The sales of José's fourth English-language album, *Souled,* reached more than a million dollars. At twenty-four years of age, José was a success by every measure. Few people today have careers that offer as much promise for the future.

Skillful at reading and writing braille, José now spends much of his time composing music. He has learned to play the banjo, bass, piano, organ, harpsichord, mandolin, harmonica, and trumpet.

José also finds time for fun. He likes to swim, ride a bicycle, play baseball, and sail.

Many people, meeting José for the first time, do not realize he is blind. This pleases him. He laughs about the time he and friends rented horses from a stable and went riding. José got a spirited horse, and when they returned to the stable, the owner nearly fainted when he was told José was blind.

José puts great stock in music as an ideal career. He says that to be a successful musician, a person must have talent, have only music on the mind, and give music everything he or she has got. Anyone who has heard José Feliciano knows he gives his music everything he's got.

CHERYL TOUSSAINT, Somebody Special

by Francene Sabin

In 1967, a group called Youth in Action held a track meet in Brooklyn, New York. Because she had nothing better to do, thirteen-year-old Cheryl Toussaint went to watch the meet that day. Sitting in the stands with her friends, Cheryl found it all very exciting: the speed of the runners, the yells and cheers of the spectators, the fun of watching the races.

While the meet officials were arranging the order of final events, an open race for girls was announced. That meant that any girl present could come to the starting line and compete even if she didn't belong to a track team. Cheryl loved to run — on the street, in the school yard, or in the local playground. She wanted to enter, but she held back.

The girls she had been watching in the meet could run so fast! Cheryl's friends teased her to give it a try. "Go ahead. Don't be chicken." And when one said, "I dare you," Cheryl accepted the challenge.

She was wearing a dress and a pair of sandals, so a friend who was wearing sneakers swapped shoes with Cheryl. Then another girl, who had changed into track shorts, lent her jeans to Cheryl.

"It was a hundred-yard dash," Cheryl remembered, "and I really didn't know what to do. I didn't even know how long a hundred yards was. I just stood at the line in one person's dungarees and another person's sneakers. I didn't know how to start; I was standing up straight. Then a man said, 'Take your marks . . . Set . . . Go!' and I ran. I came in second."

There were several qualifying heats being run, and Cheryl was told that the finals would be held shortly. As she waited, Cheryl began to wonder whether she should enter the finals. "For some reason, I began to hurt right around my hip area, and I didn't understand it. So I told my friends that I thought I wouldn't run. They began to tease me again, saying that I was a chicken and that I was dropping out because I thought I wasn't going to win. Well, that did it. I went back on the track, ran the final, and took fourth place. That wasn't bad, but the thing that got me was

that the three girls ahead of me were all Atoms. I was so impressed with how fast they could run that all I could think of was how I could join their club too."

The Atoms Track Club of Brooklyn was made up of local girls who wanted to run in races. There were many fine runners in the group, and it was beginning to develop into a real track power.

After the meet was over, Cheryl saw some Atoms runners doing exercises on the grass. Building up her courage, she walked over to them and asked how she could join the club. They told her that joining was easy: All she had to do was come to the practices every afternoon.

For a while, Cheryl went to Prospect Park in Brooklyn for the Atoms's daily practice. But when no one paid much attention to her, she began to doubt herself and the results of her running. "I thought that because I was putting my whole heart into it, the coach should have done more than tell me to run laps, do exercises, or practice starts," she said.

Cheryl had no way of knowing that Atoms Coach Fred Thompson always treated new team members this way. It was his way of testing their willingness to work. Realizing that the tough, long practice sessions were more than many people could stand, he would watch the new team members without their being aware of it. Then, if they stayed with the practice sessions without any encouragement, he would be sure that they were ready for real coaching.

After two months of practicing with the Atoms, Cheryl dropped out of the club. The memory of her one race, however, kept coming back to her — the pounding heart before the start, the wonderfully free feeling of running, the excitement of coming in ahead of some others. So after six months away from the Atoms, Cheryl Toussaint returned to the club, this time to stay.

Fred Thompson had missed Cheryl during those six months and had hoped that she would come back. He had sent a message to Cheryl telling her that she would always be welcome. He was very pleased when she did return.

The season for cross-country racing (long-distance races over all kinds of land) was just beginning, and Fred took the Atoms to a cross-country meet on Long Island, New York. That day Cheryl officially competed for the first time with the Atoms, and neither she nor the coach will ever forget it.

"Cheryl had come back to train with us for about two weeks," Fred recalled, "but I decided to enter her in a one-mile run, just to give her some racing experience. Of course, she wasn't really in condition, and I knew it. So, I said to her before the race, 'Don't go out too fast, stay with the pack, and just try to finish.'

"Well, the gun went off, and before I knew it, Cheryl was a hundred yards in front of the other girls. I said to myself, 'This kid is going to pass out!' But she just kept running. Then, with about a hundred yards to go, she just about collapsed. She fell down, then got up and started crawling on her hands and knees. It was unbelievable! She stood up, staggered some more, got about twenty yards from the finish line and fell again. She kept on going, crawling, still with nobody near her, and then right at the wire another girl caught up and won. I knew, at that moment, that Cheryl was going to be somebody very special. I had never seen anyone run like that before."

Until Fred Thompson came into her life, nobody had ever thought of Cheryl Toussaint as somebody special. Shortly after Cheryl's birth on December 16, 1952, her parents separated, and Cheryl went to live with her grandmother. In the crowded schools she attended, Cheryl slipped further and further behind grade level until, by junior-high school, she was called a "slow learner."

Then Cheryl joined the Atoms, and everything in her world, including school, took on new meaning. Fred Thompson demanded that Cheryl do better, scolded her when she let up, and praised her when she succeeded. "Freddy always encouraged all the girls and me to try for good grades," Cheryl explained. "He'd say, 'When those report cards come in, I want to see them!' and he really meant it. He made me feel that he was just as concerned with how I was doing with my studies as with my running."

At school, Cheryl set to work. She begged the school officials to let her take algebra, a foreign language, and more advanced English courses. The teachers thought that Cheryl wouldn't be able to do the work, but she insisted that they let her try. Finally, they agreed to let her carry those subjects, in addition to her other classes, on a one-year trial. It was hard work, but Cheryl gave it everything she had and began to learn and do well.

"When I got my report card," Cheryl said, "not only did I feel good for getting good grades, but I felt proud to show them to somebody who really appreciated them. Freddy would say, 'Cheryl, that's really good. Keep it up.'"

Cheryl learned that she was expected to do well in school — flunk and you were off the team — and to work out regularly on the track. She stuck with the hard, two-hour practice every day. "When I first joined the team," Cheryl remembered, "I was ex-hausted. I'd come home after practice barely able to shower and eat. All I wanted to do was sleep. My grandmother was used to the energetic, bouncy kid I had been. And here I was collapsing!"

"Even though it knocked me out, the running definitely helped me to do better in school. I had to be very well scheduled. If I hadn't been running on the track every day, I'd have been at the nearest park playing handball or softball after school. But with those early-evening practices being so tiring, I knew that I had to spend my afternoons doing homework if I wanted to graduate."

"It might sound kind of boring," Cheryl said of her teen years, "because my life was a round of sleeping, eating, classes, running, studying, and more sleeping. But I was doing what I loved and what I wanted to do. Although I had a less active social life than most girls, it didn't bother me. Only when I was sixteen did I go through a stage when I was always moaning that I wasn't going out enough and that I always had to call off my dates. Looking back, I think I just couldn't tell the difference between the important and the unimportant. Luckily, I outgrew that!"

As her schoolwork improved, so did Cheryl's performance on the track. She loved the feeling of running, and now, with Coach Thompson's faith in her and her own new image of herself, she began turning in faster times and winning races. Cheryl had been running for only about a year when she qualified to compete in the United States trials for a place on the 1968 Olympic squad.

Looking back at that time, Cheryl later said, "I had been doing fairly well, but at that point, I didn't think I was ready for the Olympics. It was enough of a thrill to know that I had made it to the trials. I ran and did the best I could, coming in fifth, but I didn't make the Olympic team. I was disappointed, but I know now that if I had qualified for the team then, it might have been bad for me. Athletes can be thrown. I've seen it happen to some when they went further than their emotional levels could handle. Success too soon isn't always a good thing. Sometimes people aren't mentally ready for things. I think I wasn't ready for the Olympics then."

Cheryl was ready to become an outstanding student, however. Fred Thompson had convinced her that she was college material and that with a little more effort she might earn a scholarship. To Cheryl, Fred Thompson's mention of college sounded like a dream. But she understood, as did all the Atoms, that Fred meant every word he said. He told them that if they were good enough, poverty would never stop

them. With that goal in sight, the "slow learner" was soon getting *A*'s and zooming to the top of her class.

In June 1970, Cheryl graduated from Eramus Hall High School in Brooklyn and received a scholarship to New York University.

Just four months earlier, Cheryl had set the first of her several world records. "It was in Toronto, Canada," she recalled, "at the Maple Leaf Invitational Indoor Games. I had never run the 600-yard event before, but I felt prepared because I had been training well.

"There were so many girls in the event that it was split into two heats, both to count as finals. That meant you could win your heat and still lose the race if the girls in the other section had faster times. I was in the second heat, and my goal was to win my heat and to beat the time of the winner in the first heat.

"There were three and three-quarter laps to run in all, and with about two laps left, I heard Freddy yelling, 'Go! Go! What are you waiting for?' And I went!

"I won my heat, then walked around the track to where Freddy and my teammates were waiting. Everybody was jumping up and down and smiling and reaching out to me. I looked at them and asked, 'Did I win?' What I meant was, did I beat the fastest time of the first heat? They just kept smiling. Then

Freddy said, 'Look up at the clock.' So I looked, and the clock read 1:22.2. I said, 'That's nice; I won.' Freddy just kept looking at me and said very calmly, 'I think it's a new world record.'

"I thought he was kidding, until it was announced over the loudspeaker. I was so excited, and I couldn't believe it. I just couldn't imagine that *I* had really broken a world record — me, who'd never run a 600-yard race before, who had never, never thought of myself as a world record holder. It was too much for me to understand. Freddy was overjoyed, and I was too. I can't even express all the feelings I had. He told me to jog a victory lap, and I went around the track crying, with my mind in a total fog. At that moment, I felt as if I'd never be tired, as if I could run forever."

Cheryl's highest athletic goal — the Olympics — became the center of her life. She even took German at college, so she could communicate in Munich, Germany, in 1972.

Cheryl's sights were set on qualifying for the 1972 Olympic team. Nothing was more important than that. Every meet counted because every race was a rehearsal for the big one. During the indoor season in the winter of 1971–1972, she was undefeated. She was faster every time out, and everything seemed to be falling into place.

Then the outdoor season began. Cheryl had to run a time outdoors that would qualify her for the United States Olympic team. She began to press and lost her concentration on the track. Coach Thompson tried to calm her, to reassure her that a good running time depended on good competition and that she would make the team. Soon she had qualified as a runner on the metric mile relay team. But she still hadn't qualified in her individual event, the 800-meter run.

Cheryl went to the Olympic training camp with just one last chance to make the team in an individual event. "On the day of the race," Fred Thompson remembered, "I sneaked in so that Cheryl wouldn't see me. I hid behind a tree and watched her run. When she qualified, I came out, and she saw me. Well, we both cried and cried with relief. It was really down to the wire on that one."

Then Cheryl was off to Munich and the 1972 Olympics. Her first event was the 800-meter run, her specialty. In the qualifying race, she followed Fred Thompson's advice never to fall farther back than third — with disastrous results. She failed to qualify and was out of the competition for the medals. "If she'd been in any other heat, what I said would have been fine," Fred said afterward. "But the girls in her race went out so fast that Cheryl was thrown off her normal pace

and didn't make it. It was my mistake, and I'll never stop blaming myself. If Cheryl had run her usual race, pacing her first quarter more slowly, she would have made it to the semifinals and then, maybe, to the finals."

The night after the race, Fred went looking for Cheryl in Olympic Village and found her in tears, broken-hearted at what she considered her failure. Fred reminded her that she was the youngest one in the event and that her running career was just beginning. Besides, the relay race was yet to come. Cheryl still had one more chance to win a medal.

On September 9, the women's 400-meter relay race was set to be run. The United States team of Mabel Ferguson, Madeline Jackson, Cheryl Toussaint, and Kathy Hammond had to do well in their race to qualify for the finals. Cheryl, running the third leg of the relay, waited to receive the baton from Madeline Jackson.

"I turned," Cheryl said, recalling the situation, "and reached for the stick. I was just starting to run with it when a girl from another team fell in front of me. My first reaction was to step back so I wouldn't trip over her. But instead, I dashed around her, only to have another runner step on the heel of my left shoe. Half of my shoe was tied on tightly, but the other half was crushed under my heel. 'Oh, no,' I thought, 'I can't believe it. Here I am in the Olympics, and my shoe is coming off!' I didn't have time to stop to pull it up. So I just ran. I went another ten yards or so when the shoe flew up in the air. I just kept running, dazed, and wondering if my shoe had hit anyone, if the people in the stands and on TV could see my bare foot, and if they were asking what that girl was doing out there without a shoe.

"There were two teams ahead of us when I got the stick, and somehow, before I knew it, I passed their runners. Then I saw where I was, and I felt stunned at getting there. All I'd been thinking was that my shoe had come off, and this was the Olympics, and that these things don't happen. But they did."

She may have done it the hard way — but she'd done it. Cheryl and her teammates made it to the relay finals. "I was really confident," Cheryl said of the finals. "Nothing more could happen after that shoe incident. So when I received the baton pass, I just ran and ran until I couldn't run any more. The United States team came in second behind East Germany.

"Getting up on the victory stand with my teammates, I realized that I was going home from my first Olympics with a silver medal. Of course, I wish our team had won, but that didn't mean I wasn't pleased to be up there on the victory stand."

Cheryl won many honors and prizes in her running career, but the greatest reward track gave her was a chance at a whole new life. For Cheryl, being one of Freddy's Atoms spelled the difference between being nobody and being somebody very special.

LYDIA'S SECRET MISSION

by Joseph and Edith Raskin

Lydia Darragh was busily making buttons for her son John's coat while the fourteen-year-old boy stood by, waiting for her to finish. Her husband, William, was thoughtfully smoking his pipe before the fireplace. Even though the November morning was spreading a chill through the room, the fire had not been lit. Wood was hard to come by, like everything else since the British had taken over their town.

The shutters of the Darraghs' windows were open. Anyone passing by, whether an officer from the British headquarters across the street or a fellow Philadelphian, was welcome to glance in on their household. Everyone knew that the Darraghs were Quakers and that, as Quakers, they were for peace and against war and violence. What nobody knew was how strongly the Darraghs disliked the British invaders.

As Lydia sewed, she tucked scraps of paper into the buttons. She thought how simple it had been so far for her to find out about the enemy's supplies and the number of troops. Whatever facts she had gathered were put into a code that William had made up. Only their son Charles, stationed with General Washington, could figure out the messages.

Once she had finished sewing the buttons on the coat, Lydia helped John into it. He looked closely at the buttons. They were neatly covered with the same material as his coat. He smiled; no one would suspect they held a secret message!

"Be careful," Lydia warned him.

"Don't worry. I've done this before, and I've never been caught, have I?" he answered confidently.

As she watched her son leave through the back door, Lydia could not help worrying. It was true that John was as hard to catch as a chipmunk. He knew every bush and hiding hole on the way to the American army. But there was always the danger of his being seen by the British patrol.

"I had best get back to my teaching," her husband said, getting up from his chair.

"Aren't thee going to wait for thy noon meal?" she called to him. But then she remembered that there was hardly any food in the house. She would have to go marketing. As she went to fetch a basket, Ann and Susannah, who had been playing in the next room, suddenly appeared, eager to be taken along. Accepting their mother's silence as approval, they quickly tied on their little bonnets.

Walking down the street between her two daughters, Lydia did not seem particularly interested in her surroundings. But her sharp eyes noticed how well clothed and well fed the British were. "Those greedy farmers!" she thought. "Just because they can get better prices, they would rather sell to the enemy and let their own people starve."

As she continued her way down the street, she counted the houses that had been left by their owners. None of these deserted houses had any drainpipes. The Patriots had taken these lead pipes to mold into bullets.

"Look, Mama!" Ann cried, pointing to an empty store.

"Another store has closed up!" Susannah chimed in.

"There's no need to shout; I can see for myself," Lydia said to quiet them. Just then, she heard someone call her name. As she turned her head, she recognized the adjutant general who was stationed at the British headquarters across the street from her house. She had spoken to the officer many times before. A chill went through her. Had something terrible happened to John?

"Are you out marketing?" he asked politely.

She smiled with relief; he was only being friendly. "Yes, I am," she answered.

"Then I hope your effort will be rewarded with a full basket," he said, giving her a parting salute.

His hopeful words proved false. After trudging up and down the streets, all Lydia could buy with her money was a bit of butter. "Well," she told her daughters, "at least we won't starve. After all, we still have some bread. And this butter melted in hot water will make a soup that should last us for the whole week."

As soon as she arrived home, she anxiously peered into all the rooms. "John couldn't possibly be back yet," she thought, trying to reassure herself. But even though she had plenty of work to do around the house, time seemed to pass much too slowly.

"Someone is knocking on the door, Mama," her older daughter, Susannah, called out.

Lydia's face paled as she opened the door. Standing there was the same adjutant general she had met on the street a while before.

"I have something to tell you," he said. As Lydia made no answer, he went on. "We find that we are short of space in our headquarters. As your house is convenient and also large, we have decided to use it for meetings of our high command. You and your family will have to leave your house at once."

"But we have no other place to go to!" Lydia protested.

"I'm sorry, but this is Commander Howe's order."

Lydia could tell from the tone of his voice that the decision was final. For a few moments, she was silent. Then, getting hold of herself, she said, "I understand your need for more space. But wouldn't my large room alone be big enough for the meetings? You would be most kind to let me keep the small room for my family. Besides, I would see to it that the house is properly kept for the meetings."

"There are five of you."

"I'll send my two daughters to stay with some relatives in the country," Lydia answered promptly.

To her surprise, the adjutant general nodded. "Not a bad arrangement. Have the room ready for us."

When her husband returned from teaching, she told him the bad news. He received it calmly. "We still have our house," he said quietly. Then he added, "Is John back?"

"Thee knows it is too early to expect him back," she said, trying to put William at ease.

All their worries disappeared when, toward sunset, they heard the back door open. It was John. He looked tired but carefree, as though he had spent the whole day playing in the yard.

"Did thee see thy brother?" Lydia asked eagerly.

"Yes, mother," John answered. "Charles is all right. General Washington has made him a lieutenant."

Lydia and her husband exchanged proud glances. But as she fingered the buttons on John's coat, she shook her head scornfully. "Thy lieutenant brother didn't do too fine a job sewing back the button coverings," she noted.

While Lydia's husband had accepted the fact that the British had taken over part of their house, it was not so with John. Lydia constantly had to pull at his sleeve to keep him from being rude to the British officers, who began to come in and out of their house as though it were a public place.

Lydia, like her husband, could accept the presence of these uninvited guests. What *did* bother her was the sudden activity she had noticed in the British headquarters.

The family was sitting in their room late one afternoon. They were whispering about what was happening across the street when they were interrupted by a loud knock. Before any of them could move, the door was thrown open, and there stood the adjutant general.

"Have the meeting room readied at once," he ordered Lydia. "My staff officers and I intend to stay up quite late. You and your family are to go to bed early. I'll wake you when we have finished."

Lydia obediently went to clean up the meeting room,

arrange the candles, and set a fire in the fireplace. Since the British had started using the room, there was always plenty of wood. As she was doing these chores, several questions raced through her mind. Why were they being sent to bed early? What secret plans would be discussed at this meeting? Were they going to attack Washington's army stationed nearby? And her son Charles — what would happen to him?

Darkness was falling when Lydia hurried William and John to bed. She stayed up long enough to admit the officers. After they arrived, Lydia lay down, fully clothed, on her bed. She was too alarmed to be able to sleep. Eager as she was to know what was going on in the meeting room, her honest Quaker nature made her hold back from eavesdropping. But her anxiety about the meeting won out. She tiptoed barefoot to a closet that had only a thin wall between it and the meeting room.

With her ear against the wall, Lydia strained to hear their voices. At first she could hear nothing. She began to fear that she was too late. Suddenly she heard the adjutant general's voice. "These are the final orders we have agreed upon," he was saying. "All our troops are to leave this city on the fourth of December of this year, 1777, and are to march out to attack the American army encamped at Whitemarsh. This is to be done in the strictest secrecy."

Shocked as she was, Lydia remained glued to the wall, hoping to hear more of their plans. There was silence, then the scraping of chairs. Realizing that the meeting was over, she hastily retreated to her room. The moment she got into bed, there was a knock on the door. Lydia pretended not to hear it. A louder knock followed; still she did nothing. After the third knock, she left her bed and, acting as if she had just awakened, she opened the door. It was the adjutant general.

"We are leaving," he told her. "You may now put out the candles and the fire and lock up the house. We will not disturb your sleep anymore tonight."

Lydia forced herself to attend to those tasks and then went back to bed. Nightmarish thoughts kept passing through her mind. Were the British planning to destroy Washington's army, killing thousands of people? And what would that do to the country? It was clear to her that General Washington had to be warned immediately of the British plan. She glanced over at her husband, who was sleeping soundly. She considered waking him up but decided against it. He would be in less danger if he knew nothing.

In the morning, she told her husband that she was out of flour and was going to the mill at Frankford.

"It's a long distance, Lydia. Then there is the British line to cross. I will not let thee go alone," William protested.

"I'll be all right," Lydia answered. Before he could argue further, she left the house and crossed the street to British headquarters. Being a familiar figure to the guard, she had no trouble getting in to see General Howe.

"What can I do for you?" the general asked, clearly amused by the sight of the plainly dressed Quaker with a sack under her arm.

"I need a pass through your lines to get to the mill at Frankford," she said simply.

The general studied her, but Lydia calmly met his gaze. She knew that the British had been allowing civilians to cross British lines to attend to their affairs. Why, then, was the general hesitating? Had she given him cause not to trust her? She held her breath. Finally, she saw a faint smile appear on the general's face.

"You've been helpful to us, and we appreciate your kindness, Mrs. Darragh," General Howe said, handing her a permit. "I see no reason why you should not go to Frankford. Just be sure that's all you do."

Lydia thanked him and promptly started on her five-mile journey to the mill. Now and then, she was stopped by British guards. But, possibly because of her simple Quaker manner and clothes, they barely glanced at her permit and let her go.

When she reached the mill, she left her flour sack to be filled. Then, without taking time to rest, she hurried westward along the stretch of land that lay between the two armies. There was always the danger of being hit by a stray bullet from either side, but Lydia walked purposefully on. She had only one thought — to meet someone from the American lines. At last, seeing a group of soldiers riding toward her, she slowed down.

"Well," she decided, "if they are British, I will tell them that I'm on my way to see my daughters, who are staying with relatives." Her face lit up when she saw that the riders were in fact American scouts. Not only that, but one of the soldiers was Craig, who was a close friend of the Darragh family.

"Mrs. Darragh!" Craig exclaimed, galloping over to her. "What are you doing so far from home?"

"Get down from your horse and walk with me a bit," she urged. "I have something important to tell you."

When they were a safe distance from the rest of the riders, Lydia told Craig what she had overheard at the secret meeting. She begged him not to pass on the information to anyone except General Washington for fear that it might harm her family.

"I promise," Craig said gravely. Then he mounted his horse and galloped off toward the American lines.

Having done what she had set out to do, Lydia returned to the mill to pick up her sack of flour. No one paid much attention to the Quaker woman bent under the burden of a heavy sack. Even William and John suspected nothing when, on her return, Lydia quietly busied herself around the house.

She did not sleep well that night. She kept hearing the sound of footsteps and the clatter of horses' hoofs. The British army was leaving on its secret expedition.

The next few days seemed to drag on endlessly for Lydia. Now and then she would look out the window, hoping to learn something about what was happening at Whitemarsh. At last, on the eighth of December, she saw the British soldiers marching back into the city in orderly formation. They looked as fresh as when they had left. What had happened?

She was sitting at the window trying to figure it out when suddenly the adjutant general burst into the room.

"I wish to speak to you, Mrs. Darragh," he said sternly. "Come with me to the conference room."

Lydia followed him into the room. He closed the door, locked it, and turned to stare at her. Then he asked, "Was any of your family up the night that I met with my officers?"

She returned his stare calmly, even though she was filled with fear for herself and for her family. "No," she answered firmly. "They all went to sleep early."

"Strange, very strange," the adjutant general muttered, looking puzzled. "You, I know, were fast asleep. I had to knock on your door three times before you heard me. Yet I am sure that someone must have told Washington about our plans. Impossible, simply impossible." He looked angry now. "On arriving near the enemy's lines, we found their cannons mounted and their troops so prepared to receive us that we had to leave without fighting. It made us look ridiculous."

After the adjutant general had stormed out, Lydia let out a sigh of relief. She had not even been forced to lie to the man. With a smile on her face, the plainly dressed Quaker woman went back to her work.

BICYCLE STYLES:
Yesterday
and Today

by Stephen Henkel

According to one meaning, a bicycle is "a vehicle with two wheels, one behind the other; a steering handle; a saddle seat; and pedals by which it is driven." If it has three wheels or one, it's not a bicycle. If the wheels are side by side instead of in front and back, it's not a bicycle. If it has no pedals, or if it is driven by a motor, it's not a bicycle.

Who invented such a thing as the bicycle in the first place? There were bicyclelike machines before 1800, but none met the meaning given above. The earliest-known picture of something like a bicycle can be seen in a stained-glass window, dated 1642, in a church in England. But nobody knows if the machine pictured was real or imagined by the artist, or even if it had two wheels. Around 1690, the Comte de Sivrac of France invented

a two-wheeled vehicle called a Walk-along. The rider drove it by sitting on a saddle and pushing the ground with her or his feet. Several kinds of walk-alongs were in use by the late 1700's.

Another early forerunner of the bicycle was built in 1816 by Baron Karl von Drais of Germany. Called the Draisine, it was made of wood. The Draisine was different from the earlier walk-along in one important way: The front wheel turned, allowing the rider to steer the machine. In 1818 and 1819, Dennis Johnson of London made two kinds of Draisines — one for men and one for women. There was a cross bar on the men's model but not on the women's. This difference between men's and women's bicycles remains unchanged after more than a century and a half. Machines like Johnson's were known by several names, such as Hobbyhorse, Swift-walker, and Dandy Horse.

Bicyclelike machines improved steadily after these first inventions. In 1840, Kirkpatrick MacMillan of Scotland added cranks similar to foot pedals to the front of his hobbyhorse. The cranks were connected to the rear wheel by rods. MacMillan is often called the true inventor of the bicycle.

In 1861, in France, the bicycle underwent another change. Two brothers named Michaux joined pedals to the front wheel. This bicycle had wooden wheels and iron tires. Because the ride was usually quite rough, the machine was known as the Boneshaker. In 1868, solid rubber tires replaced the iron ones, making the ride a little smoother.

In 1870, a bicycle called the Penny Farthing, the High-wheeler, or the Ordinary appeared in England. On this bicycle, the rider sat on a seat that was over a large front wheel. As time went on, the front wheel was made bigger and bigger for more speed. By the 1880's, front wheels of about fifty inches across and rear wheels of about seventeen inches across were common. These bicycles were usually heavy, weighing fifty to seventy-five pounds. But some weighed as much as one hundred fifty pounds and others as little as twenty-one pounds.

About this time, a man named Oldreive carried the big-wheel idea to an extreme. He came up with a huge-wheeled tricycle. The rider for this machine had to sit *inside the wheel* to pedal.

During this same period, there were some people who made bicycles with smaller front wheels and placed the seat closer to the back wheel, which gave the rider a safer position. Singer's Xtraordinary, also known as the Dwarf Safety Velocipede, is an example of this kind.

From 1885 to 1890, several more changes were made to the bicycle. In 1885, J. K. Starley of England brought out the Rover. It had wheels of the same size, a chain-driven rear wheel, and solid rubber tires. Then three years later, James Dunlop of Ireland came forth with air-filled tires. By the beginning of the 1890's, a bicycle called the Safety had two twenty-eight-inch wheels, a chain drive, and air-filled tires. The Safety became a popular bicycle, and it was the model for the modern diamond-frame bicycle. Since the 1890's, only small changes have been made to the bicycle.

Today, the most common bicycle is the Touring Model, also called the English Racer. But other models are being designed and are gaining in popularity, such as the High-rise. There is even a bicycle that folds, making it easy to carry and store. Bicycles come in a wide range of shapes, sizes, and weights. Take your pick! And welcome to the world of pedal power!

The Blue Bike

by John Savage

Her bicycle was really great. George first saw it at a youth hostel in the Glen of Aherlow, County Tipperary in Ireland. It was leaning against a wall of mossy stones, between the kitchen and the well. George dropped both buckets to admire it.

One thing he'd seen plenty of this summer was bicycles. It seemed as if half the college students of America — including, of course, himself — had been spending the vacation parking bikes outside the youth hostels of Europe.

But no one had a bicycle like this. The frame was a female model, painted shiny forget-me-not blue. The spokes and handlebars gleamed in the misty sunshine. And the saddle bags were made of the finest leather. And look at all those speeds! The sprockets were piled up like griddle cakes. That meant a dozen forward speeds, at least. If she did her shifting right, she could climb the side of Dublin Castle!

He sighed, picked up the buckets, and went to the well across the road. Anyway, it was a nice morning. A thrush hopped ahead of him, flipping its tail. A wood pigeon kept making a five-word announcement — coo-roo, coo-roo, roo — from a treetop. The cows were mooing in their shed, out in back.

Nobody else was up. George had sneaked out of the men's dormitory without waking the German medical student or the Pakistani guitar

135

player. He'd tiptoed through the Common Room, past the closed door of the women's dormitory, and down the stairs. Now he filled the two buckets at the well. He couldn't help wondering about the owner of that bike.

He carried the buckets back to the kitchen, still thinking about the blue bike. He'd gone to bed early last night, having ridden all the way from the Foulksrath hostel, with a long stop at the Rock of Cashel. He hadn't seen any women here at Ballydavid Wood last night, except for the warden herself. So the woman with the fancy bike must have turned up after he'd gone to bed. . . . Well, that was one thing he knew about her, at least: She was the night-owl type.

He didn't really *care* about her, but it would be sort of interesting if she would come down to fix her breakfast before he had to leave. She didn't, as it turned out. At six A.M., which was the earliest the warden would let anyone use the hostel kitchen, he fried his bacon and eggs. The German medical student came down, yawning, just as George finished washing up. Nobody else came.

After breakfast George went upstairs to fold the blankets he'd used. By the time he'd done that, the warden was up and about. George told her he'd like to do his chores early and hit the road, so she had him sweep the Common Room. Then she gave him back his card. He climbed into his back pack rather slowly, but the owner of the blue bicycle didn't show up. The blue bomb was still parked against the wall. He'd never know the owner. He shook the rain off his bicycle and rode away.

The ride to Caher, through a mild drizzle of rain, took him an hour. He turned right, at the three-way intersection, and headed for Cork. Between Caher and Kilbeheny, he came to a long uphill stretch, over the shoulder of the Galtee Mountains. It was on that stretch that he first saw the blue bike in motion.

He was puffing along, pedaling hard. A woman with golden hair passed him so fast that he hardly knew what was happening. Her "Morning!" floated back to him in a voice as soft as a wood pigeon's, and then she got smaller as she disappeared in the distance up the hill.

Her legs, in green ski pants, were moving easily and fast. (His own were grinding along very slowly because he had only one speed.) She wasn't wearing a back pack. That would be because she had saddle bags.

By the time he got over the hill, she was out of sight. He stopped for lunch at Mitchelstown, spent some of the afternoon at Moore Park House, and pedaled up to the Cork hostel at nine P.M. Her bike was outside, but she had already eaten and gone to bed.

So she wasn't a night owl after all. She was changeable; that was it. And she had too many speeds. He'd never know who she was.

He failed to see her the next morning because he needed an early start to make Killarney. It was sad, somehow, but at least the day was beautiful.

That was the day she passed him in the Derrynasaggart Mountains, on the Kerry border. He'd been sort of listening for her, but her bike was just too quiet. She sang out "Hi!" and he sang out "Wait!" But she had already gone.

At the Killarney hostel, Aghadoe House, he got a good look at her at last. Or anyway, he *hoped* the woman he was looking at was the one. There were several complications. Aghadoe House is almost the biggest hostel in the country. There were thirty or forty bikes outside. One of the bikes was hers.

In the dining room that night, an American woman with green ski pants and golden hair taught a group of French children to make folded-paper birds that would flap their wings if their tails were pulled. George stood at the edge of the group, not wanting to interrupt. French children never sleep. By ten P.M., she was showing them how to make a turtle, and George had to get some rest for the long day ahead. If he fell behind schedule, he'd miss his ship. He didn't sleep right away though. He lay in an upper bunk with his eyes open, starting to correct the picture in his head; slim and friendly, loves children, surely the quiet type.

The next day, she passed him between Knocknagashel and Kilkinlea.

That night, through a stone wall a foot thick, he heard

her singing "Old Dan Tucker" for a dormitory full of Irish girls — quiet, my foot.

On the day after that, he had an accident. At least he could *say* it was an accident. He'd been looking back over his shoulder, and his bike happened to tip over, and he happened to skin his knee. The woman on the blue bike happened to be a hundred yards behind him. She'd been gaining fast, but, of course, she stopped.

"I think it's broken," George said without getting up.

She looked at his leg and smiled. "I don't." She got a tidy, little first-aid kit out of one of her saddle bags and swabbed his knee with something cold.

"You're the motherly type," George told her.

"I'm not a type at all. At least I hope not." She put away the kit, stepped gracefully astride the blue bomb, and left him lying there. Her parents must have told her not to stand around talking with strange men.

He got on his bike and rode on toward Ennis. This was to be his last full day in Ireland.

That evening he got lost, a few miles west of Kinvara, in County Galway. By the time he spotted the triangular sign for Doorus House, it was almost ten. The blue bike was there, leaning against a tree, but its owner had gone to bed. George gave the warden his card and small fee, ate a can of beans, and hit the sack.

He got up after seven the next morning because he didn't have far to ride to catch his ship. There wasn't anybody in the kitchen, so he tried the dining room. It was full of people he didn't know. He looked out the window. The blue bike was still there. Maybe, if he stalled a bit, he and the woman could fix breakfast together.

He was reading the plaque over the fireplace when he heard somebody on the stairs.

She came past the door and went straight out into the sunshine. George followed her to the blue bike. "That's the nicest bicycle I've ever seen. How many speeds?"

"Fifteen." She smiled. "I've never used them all." She wheeled the bike into the driveway.

George was startled. "You leaving already?"

She nodded, and the sun did something nice to her

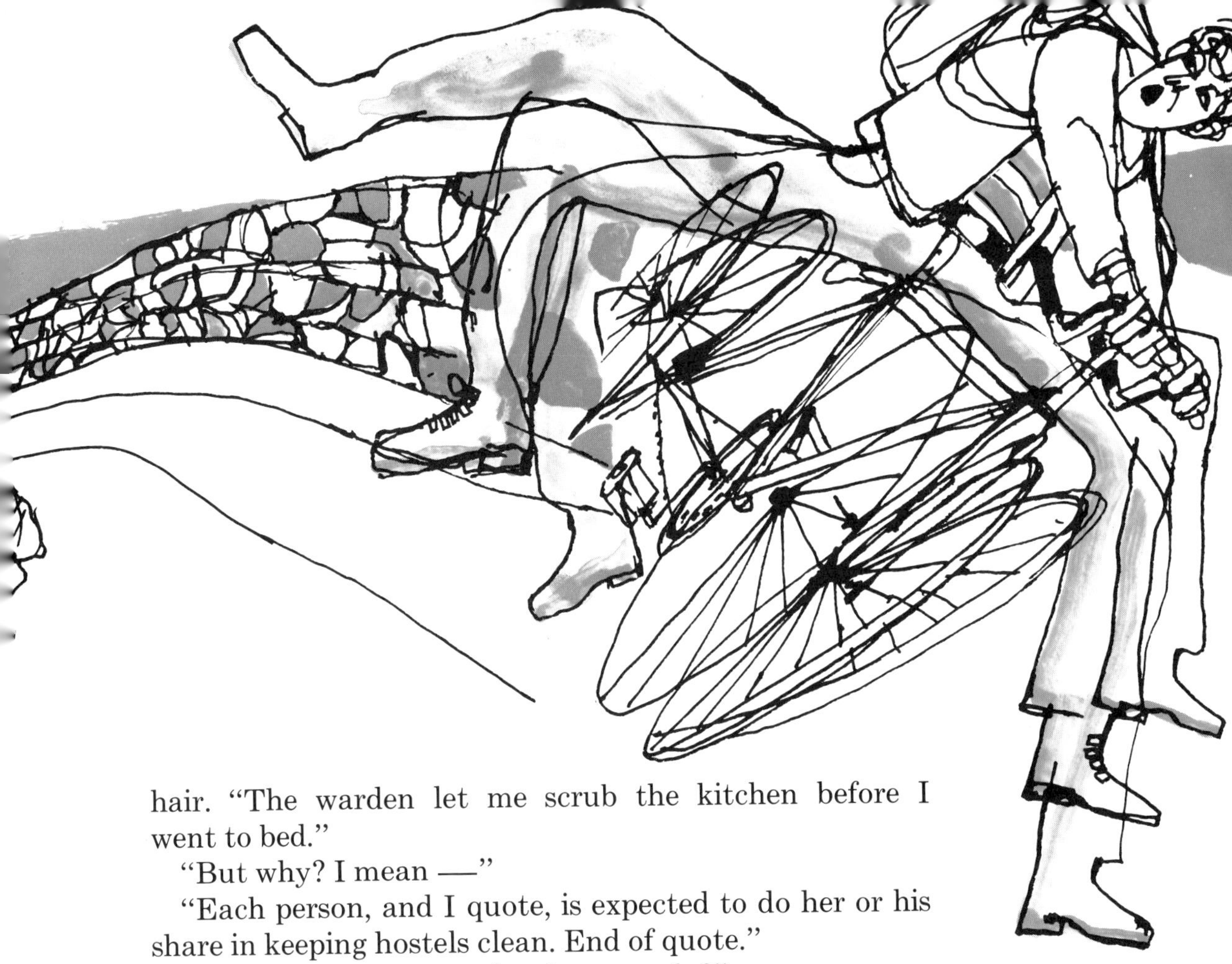

hair. "The warden let me scrub the kitchen before I went to bed."

"But why? I mean —"

"Each person, and I quote, is expected to do her or his share in keeping hostels clean. End of quote."

"I meant, why are you leaving so early?"

"I have to get to Galway," she said. "My ship sails from there at two, and I've got to do some shopping. 'Bye."

George let her go. For one thing, he hadn't had breakfast or done his chores.

For a second thing, and a grand thing it was, he was due in Galway at two himself. He had a ship to catch. It could hardly be a different ship because not many liners came this way.

Humming to himself, he strolled in to fix breakfast. It was sort of nice to be going home.

Why doesn't a bike stand up by itself?

Because it's two tired.

Survival Skill
Understanding Bicycle Safety

Perhaps you are one of the millions of people who has found that the bicycle is your favorite way to travel. If you ride a bicycle, you must obey all traffic rules — just as you should if you were driving a car.

Before you ride your bicycle, you should check the laws that your state, city, or town may have that govern bicycle riding. You may need to have the bicycle inspected, registered, or licensed before you ride it.

Next, you should be certain that the bicycle is the right size for you and that it is in good working order. It is important to have brakes, gears, and a bell or a horn that work. If you plan to carry packages, you should have a carrier on the bicycle.

When you ride a bicycle, always be sure that you can be seen. During the daytime hours, wear bright-colored clothing or attach a red or orange flag on a long pole to the bicycle. Do not ride at night unless you have to. If you must ride after dark, what should you wear? Yes, you should wear light-colored clothing. Also, you should have a light on the front and a reflector on the back of the bicycle so that you can be seen easily.

On which side of the road should you ride? Yes, you should always ride on the right with the traffic, never against it. If you have to ride on a heavily traveled street, pedal as close to the curb as possible. When you are riding with others, should you keep in a single line? Yes, you should. Two people riding beside each other take up too much road space, and the person on the outside risks being hit by an automobile. If for some reason you cannot ride your bicycle in the street, *walk* along beside it on the sidewalk. *Riding* on sidewalks is not allowed in most places.

Bicycle Safety Tips

1. Check your state and local laws.
2. Keep your bicycle in good working order.
3. Be sure you can be seen.
4. Ride on the right side of the road and in a single line.
5. Obey traffic signs and signals.
6. Give proper hand signals.
7. Stay alert and use common sense.

Like the driver of a car, the bicycle rider must obey all traffic signs and signals. Many bicycle accidents occur because a rider fails to obey these signs and signals. You know that a red light means "stop," that a green light means "go," and that you cannot go the wrong way down a one-way street.

There are several traffic signs that apply only to bicycle riders. Look at the three signs below. The first sign on the left indicates a bicycle path. How do you know that? Yes, the sign has the words BIKE ROUTE on it. Whenever you see this sign, use the special bicycle path to avoid heavy traffic. Look at the middle sign. What do you think it means? The sign shows that bicycles are not allowed on this road. This sign is often found on roads leading to highways, expressways, and toll roads. The sign on the right reminds the bicycle rider to stay on the right side of the road.

As the driver of a bicycle, you must warn other drivers behind you if you plan to make a turn or stop. Use your left arm and hand for all signals.

Look at the hand signals that are shown on this page. What position should your left arm and hand be in to indicate a left turn? Yes, your left arm and hand should be out straight. When you plan to make a left turn across traffic, observe all traffic signs, then get off your bicycle and push it across the street. Many accidents happen at crossroads, and you do not want to be involved in one of them. How should you show that you are going to make a right turn? Your left arm should be bent with the hand up. To show that you are going to slow down or stop, you should bend your left arm with the hand pointing down.

When you are bicycling in cities and towns, give a signal one hundred feet before turning or stopping. If you are bicycling in the country, give a signal two hundred feet before turning or stopping.

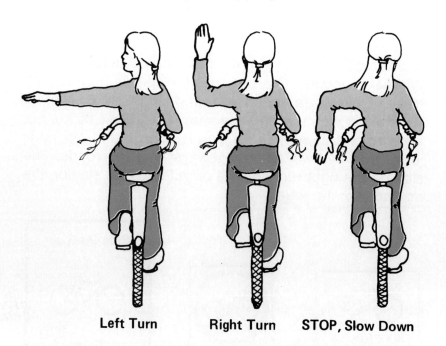

Left Turn   Right Turn   STOP, Slow Down

At all times, stay alert and use common sense. You should always watch for people walking. They have the right of way. If you have to ride beside parked cars, watch for car doors opening or cars suddenly pulling into traffic. As you bicycle along the road, watch for bumps, holes, sand, and gravel. These things can cause you to skid or to be thrown from your bicycle.

When you ride a bicycle, keep these safety tips in mind. Bicycling can be fun and a safe way to travel.

Now use what you have learned about bicycle safety to answer each of the following items. Use a separate piece of paper. Write the number of each item and the letter of the correct answer.

1. When riding after dark, you should
    a. have a light on the front of your bicycle.
    b. have a reflector on the back of your bicycle.
    c. wear light-colored clothing.
    d. do *a*, *b*, and *c* above.

2. If you have to ride a bicycle on a heavily traveled street, you should
    a. stay as close to the curb as possible.
    b. pedal beside another person.
    c. ride on the sidewalk.

3. One-way traffic signs are meant for
    a. cars and bicycles.
    b. cars only.
    c. bicycles only.

4. Marcel is riding his bicycle and wants to make a right turn. He should signal by
    a. holding his left arm and hand out straight.
    b. holding his right arm bent with his hand up.
    c. holding his right arm and hand out straight.
    d. holding his left arm bent with his hand up.

5. Roxanne is at a busy crossroads, and she has signaled to make a left turn. Now she should
    a. get off her bicycle and push it across the street.
    b. cross with the people walking while still riding her bicycle.
    c. ride across the street as quickly as she can.

ROBERTO

by Oscar Lewis

When I was about eleven years old and still in the first grade, I ran away from home for the first time. I went to Veracruz with no more than the clothes on my back. I had no money to start out with. In those days, I never had a whole peso in my pocket all at once. I was limited to the five centavos my father put under my pillow each morning before he went to work. On Sundays, I got twenty centavos. But I usually spent all my money right away and never had any left. On the road, all the money I had was a few centavos a kindly truck driver gave me.

My excuse for running away was that my father scolded me, and in reality, he always did scold me. However, the real reason was that I heard some boys talking about their adventures, and I wanted an adventure myself. So I decided to go to Veracruz. I chose that place because I had been to Veracruz once before with my family.

Gulf of Mexico

Mexico City
⊗ Texcoco
Los Reyes
Puebla
Veracruz

I walked along the highway as far as Los Reyes. I have always liked walking along a road. I like to walk day and night, until I fall down with exhaustion, and sleep at the side of the highway.

On the highway, I felt happy and carefree. The problem of food didn't worry me. It was easy for me to go up to a shack and ask for work to do in exchange for a bite to eat. Everybody gave me something to do: draw water from the well, chop wood, or any simple chore like that. Then they'd give me something to eat. Lots of people would tell me to sit down to eat first, and then they wouldn't let me do anything for them. Sometimes the people would fix up a pack of *tortillas* and salt for me to take on the road, and off I'd go.

I had laid out a route and went as I had planned. For a long while, no car would stop for me, even though they saw I was a kid. Finally a bus picked me up, and the driver asked where I was from. If I had known that saying I was from Mexico City closed doors, I would have said that I was from somewhere else. Some people from the capital have a very bad reputation. At the carnivals and *fiestas,* whenever people are caught for doing something wrong, they often turn out to be from there. . . .

I traveled alone. I never wanted to have friends go with me because I have always preferred to be on my own. It is easier for me to get around by myself. I would ask people the way. By asking, I could learn my way to anyplace.

When I left home, I felt as though a great weight was lifted off me. To live with other people is hard. I thought I never wanted to be tied to the family again. Sometimes I would ask for lodging for a night, and I would stay with a family for a few days. But I wasn't comfortable because what I was looking for was to be free. And so I went, like the air, without difficulty, without direction, free. . . . People would ask, "Why did you leave home?"

"Because my father scolded me. I have a stepmother," I always answered. How I used Elena as an excuse! I think that was why I was always making her mad so that I could use her as an excuse. I got what I wanted for the moment. I call myself a scoundrel because I used another person to cover up for me. What I have gone through is nothing compared to what I deserve.

Like all adventurers, when I arrived in Veracruz, I asked the way to the sea. I reached it and sat on a navy dock, looking at it all day. The sea was beautiful, overpowering. I saw how the guards, who watch the docks and the cargoes, had nothing else to do but fish. When it was nightfall, I wondered where I would sleep. That was not a big problem there because it was very hot. I decided to stay on one of the beaches, the best and softest one. I slept some distance from the water because of the rise of the tide.

The next day, I felt like eating. The day before, I hadn't eaten anything because I was so fascinated by watching the sea and the fishing. I went back to the docks because the cargo boats were anchored there. I saw a lot of people, a rough, husky bunch, walking back and forth. I approached the boat cook and asked if he had any work for me to do in exchange for a bite to eat. He felt sorry for me, and it was because of that cook that I got a job as a dock worker for the first time in my life. I carried small packages, and in return, I was given meals. I started work at eight in the morning and stopped at noon, then began at twelve-thirty and quit at four-thirty. I was also given permission to sleep on one of the cargo boats.

After a while, the setup didn't look as good to me as before. A boat would come in, and I would stick to it like glue. But the next day, it would pull out, and I would be homeless and without food again. I was continually looking for a place to eat and sleep. But I learned that if anybody died of starvation, it was probably due to laziness. I helped the people fishing on the free beaches pull in their nets, and instead of money, they'd give me some of their catch. In one casting, they'd get all kinds of fish. I sold most of my fish, keeping just one or two, which I'd ask someone to cook for me.

I was willing to work at whatever came along so I could eat. I never earned money working. I was given fruit, for the most part, and I even ate wild greens. When ships came in from Tabasco or from places where fruit is grown, I had a feast day! There were times, however, when I didn't taste bread for two whole weeks.

I began to worry about sleeping on the beach because I heard that the police van was going around the beaches. Anyone found sleeping on the sand was taken to jail. Nothing happened to me, but I slept with less calm, so I decided to leave the beach and head toward the mountains. I didn't dare go away from the docks in the daytime — they were the source of life for me.

I passed three months in this manner. Then, the time came when I felt like going home. I thought of my family only once in a while, but when I did, I felt like getting back home as fast as I could. There were moments when I felt brave enough to return; then I would lose heart because I thought I would be punished. I never wrote home. I didn't know how to write a letter, and I didn't want them to know where I was. I imagined that if my pa found out, he would come to get me and punish me. That is what I thought, but I went home anyway.

The return trip was hard because I had to walk from Veracruz to Puebla. It took me eight or nine days. I walked all the way as no one stopped to pick me up. I took the road that went through Córdoba and arrived at the police booth at the entrance of the city of Puebla. Because my shoes — strong miners' boots that my father always bought for me — were all worn-out, I asked some truck drivers for a lift to Mexico City, but they refused me. Some of them made fun of me. I paid no attention to them, but for the first time, I felt lonely, as lonely as a feather flying through the air. I sat at the side of the road, crying.

Finally, a police officer noticed and questioned me. He stopped a truck and said, "Take care of this kid adventurer. He's headed for Mexico City." I thanked the officer, got into the truck, and finally arrived late at night at the Merced Market, near the Zócalo, the central square of Mexico City. Imagine, I had been to Veracruz but had never seen the Zócalo! When I crossed in front of the National Palace, I was looking at the great big clock in the cathedral as it struck three o'clock in the morning. There I was, all alone in the great plaza. I hurried home, knocked at the neighborhood gate, and the gatekeeper let me in.

Outside our front door I sat, wondering whether or not to go inside. I expected a terrific scolding from Pa. I started to knock but sat down again. But I was very tired, so I got up my courage and knocked on the door.

My father opened the door in his night clothes. "So you finally got back, son. Well, come on in." He was so nice. I thought he would give me the hiding of the ages. But he said to me, "Did you have any supper?" We had no kerosene stove then, just a charcoal brazier in which he lit a fire. He heated some beans and coffee and said, "Eat. When you are finished, turn out the light." Then he went back to bed. As I knew that he left for work early and that he was a light sleeper, I turned out the light and ate in the dark. Then I went to sleep. . . . He hadn't even scolded me.

FACES

by Sara Teasdale

People that I meet and pass
    In the city's broken roar,
Faces that I lose so soon
    And have never found before,

Do you know how much you tell
    In the meeting of our eyes,
How ashamed I am, and sad
    To have pierced your poor disguise?

Secrets rushing without sound,
    Crying from your hiding places —
Let me go, I cannot bear
    The sorrow of the passing faces.

People in the restless street,
    Can it be, oh, can it be
In the meeting of our eyes,
    That you know as much of me?

The Rolling Scones

by Jane Williams Dugel

Wait a minute while I dry my hands and get away from this hot stove. There! You'd never believe to look at me that I am president of Rolling Scones, Inc. I mean, how many presidents do you discover in a kitchen? Not many, I can tell you. Now let me stir this soup once more, and then I'll tell you how all this happened.

Frankie Flake, this friend of mine, started the whole thing one dark day several years ago when she signaled me to meet her after class.

"Listen, I need help badly," she breathed. We were standing in front of my locker stuffing potato chips into our mouths. "I told Mrs. Chisholm, who lives near us, that I'd help her with a dinner party tonight. I must have been out of my mind when I said I'd do it. I can't cook! I never get into the kitchen at home. Let me tell you, coming from a family of twelve has its drawbacks."

"What do you want me to do?" I asked Frankie.

"Come with me. I called Mrs. Chisholm this morning and asked if I could bring someone along to help."

"Why me?" I asked.

"You're my friend," Frankie muttered as she ate another potato chip. "And you know something about cooking, kitchens, and food."

"So do you," I said.

"Eating, yes. Cooking, no."

We arrived at the Chisholms' house at five o'clock. "You can start by making some radish flowers, Frankie," Mrs. Chisholm said, tossing some bunches of radishes onto the counter. Then she went with me into the dining room to explain how she wanted the table set.

After a while, I ducked into the kitchen for some silver-ware. There was poor Frankie bent over the counter with lots of funny-looking little objects in front of her. I saw that she had taken the radishes, still dirty and untrimmed, and had stuck toothpicks into the bottoms of them. "I thought they might look like flower stems," she whispered hoarsely. "What do you think? Do they look like radish flowers?"

"Look," I said, "go into the dining room. At each table setting, put a fork on the left and a knife on the right." It would be easier to do the radishes myself than try to explain it to Frankie.

"Fork, left. Knife, right," I heard her repeating as I dived into the mess on the counter.

"Fork, left; fork, left," Frankie was still muttering as she rushed through the swinging door into the dining room — and crashed into Mr. Chisholm, who had just come home from the office.

We helped him to his feet and picked up his papers, the flowers he had brought, his hat, his briefcase, his coat, and the newspaper. He seemed rather stunned. Finally he spoke.

"Who . . . are . . . you?" he said slowly. I thought he sounded dangerous. Frankie cleared her throat.

"Your wife, Mrs. Chisholm . . ."

"I know her name," he said.

"Hired us. To help. Get dinner. To stir things."

"To stir things," he repeated.

"To make radish flowers," I said softly.

"To put forks on the left," Frankie whispered. "Your wife . . ."

"Mrs. Chisholm," he sighed. He took a deep breath, closed his eyes, and opened them again. Then he said, "You people must have names."

"Oh, yes," I said. "Oh, yes, indeed." I swallowed.

I should tell you at this point that the reason I know Frankie so well is alphabetical. We're always given places side by side in school. I mean, her last name is Flake, and you're not going to believe it, but mine is Flak. You don't believe it? That's all right. No one does.

"We are Frankie Flake and Frannie Flak, sir."

Mr. Chisholm just stood there staring at us. Finally he asked in a very, very quiet voice, "Where is my wife, Mrs. Chisholm?" We pointed upstairs.

The dinner went off very well. I didn't do that much of the cooking, but Frankie did a surprisingly good job of table setting once she figured out which side was left and which side was right. Anyway, we both kept busy, and Frankie found a lot to eat. But Mr. Chisholm always looked uneasy whenever one of us came near him. He had an ugly bruise on his forehead from the swinging door.

When the party was over, Mrs. Chisholm said, "I'll be glad to recommend you to my friends, if you're interested in this sort of thing. You two were great! I really enjoyed my own party!"

Something stirred in my mind. This job really had been fun, and it was a nice switch from baby-sitting or lawn mowing. Maybe if I could learn a little more about real cooking and Frankie could manage to handle the table end of things . . .

Frankie and I decided to ask Cathy Schneider to join us so that we could have two in the kitchen and one to take care of setting the table. Frankie was in charge of the last job, of course.

We had our first meeting several days after the dinner

at the Chisholms' house. "We'll have to have a name," Cathy said when we had ironed out the details. "That way people will remember us. Like . . . like . . ."

"I know," I said. "Something catchy. Something with food in it. Something like . . . Rolling Scones!"

Our business was born. We selected officers, and I became president. Cathy offered to be treasurer, since she can add and subtract quite easily. That left Frankie, who said, "I'll be the rank and file."

I was never busier than I was the next few weeks. Cathy and I spent days studying cookbooks and hanging around my father, who is a pretty good cook. He taught us how to prepare sauces, cheese and egg dishes, gelatin, rolls, stew, and roasts. You name it — we made it. Meanwhile, Frankie was supposed to be learning plain and fancy table setting, napkin folding, and flower arranging.

We finally felt ready to put a small ad in the local newspaper:

ROLLING SCONES, INC.
Flak, Flake, and Schneider
Catering — Cooking

We listed rates and phone numbers, then crossed our fingers and waited. A week later, we got our first job.

In the next few months, we worked brunches, two major dinner parties, three midnight buffets (Frankie went to sleep at each one), and a large Saturday bridge luncheon. Our fame was growing.

"Frannie? A Mrs. Chisholm called me," Cathy's voice came over the telephone. "She needs a special dinner done on the nineteenth. She says that you and Frankie have been there before."

"Oh, yes," I said, remembering our first catering job. I wondered if that bruise on Mr. Chisholm's forehead had ever gone away. "Sure, the nineteenth is free."

"It's Harry's big boss, Mr. Van Welles, and his wife," Mrs. Chisholm told us when we arrived. "He's the top man in the New York City office. He's deciding what to do with the local office this week. He's thinking about closing it down. But that means that Harry would lose his job! So Harry has spent the last week selling Mr. Van Welles on the great future of this town." She rattled on in a worried way and finally went upstairs to put the children to bed. Cathy and I started preparing the food in the kitchen. Nearby, Frankie was folding napkins.

Suddenly, at 5:50 P.M., there was what I can best describe as a squeaking/creaking/crashing/sloshing sound. Before our eyes, the kitchen ceiling fell down in slow motion, bringing with it wallpaper, rubber ducks, tile, plaster, and gallons of hot water. Screams sounded from above, and the lights went out.

"Uh . . . did you notice something?" Frankie whispered.

That brought us to life.

"Get upstairs, quick!" Cathy told Frankie. "Frannie," she told me, "get mops. Pick up the plaster. I'll throw the main switch!" and she went off in search of the fuse box. I was picking up plaster when I heard Frankie shout from upstairs that Mrs. Chisholm was hurt.

"I'm so sorry," Mrs. Chisholm moaned. She was sitting in the upstairs hall near the bathroom door in a pool of water. "My son Teddy left the bath water running — for hours, from the look of things. I opened the bathroom door, and water came pouring out. I guess the plaster had soaked through; anyway, everything went. That's when I slipped and twisted my ankle."

Cathy went to clean up the kitchen. Frankie herded the three children into a bedroom and telephoned one of her sisters to come and take care of them for the evening. I helped Mrs. Chisholm to her bed and tried to calm her down about the big dinner.

"Don't worry," I said. "We have not yet begun to fight!"

Flak, Flake, and Schneider huddled together and hatched battle plans. Then Frankie got on the phone again and lined up her brothers and sisters to help.

I was in the kitchen a little later, working by the light of a gas camp lantern that one of the Flakes had brought. I had things simmering on two camp stoves that another of the numerous Flakes had brought. Those Flakes are good people to have on your side.

"What . . . are . . . you . . . doing?" growled a deep, familiar voice from the open kitchen door.

I whirled around, knocking a bowl to the floor. Mr. Chisholm stood staring at me as if he were having a bad dream. He clutched his coat, hat, and case to his chest. Before I could say anything, he spoke again. "YOU. Don't tell me Snipp, Snapp, and Snurr, or whatever your names are, have returned." His eyes slowly traveled to the large hole in the ceiling. Then he noticed the wet piles of debris on the floor, the gas lamps, the camp stoves, wet mops, and the broken bowl. He leaned against the wall and groaned, "My big night . . ."

"Your wife . . ." I began.

"I know, I know. Mrs. Chisholm."

" . . . has been hurt," I snapped angrily. "Don't just stand there. Go up and help her get dressed, for goodness sake. You're in my way!"

Well, once again we served a lovely dinner in the Chisholm home. It was lit entirely by candlelight and fire-place light. Mrs. Chisholm looked very nice hopping around on one foot, and she managed to play the gracious hostess through clenched teeth. Mr. Chisholm seemed to like the food we'd made. As for the Van Welleses — well, I never saw two people enjoy them-selves more! They loved the candlelight (never knowing the reason for it). In fact, I even heard Mr. Van Welles say that he had not spent such a *unique* evening in years. I think Mr. Chisholm actually smiled, but I'm not sure.

Well, that's it. That's the story. Mr. Chisholm not only kept his job, but a few months later, he was transferred to New York City to the position of vice president of the main office. Vice president in charge of *ideas*.

But whenever the Chisholms want an extra special ca-tering job done, they send for Flak, Flake, and Schneider. As Mr. Chisholm says, we put him where he is today. And he feels we always give him *ideas*.

Orin Remembers

by Mary Stolz

For as long as Orin Woodward could remember, waking up was always hard. Even on summer mornings, when the world was touched with bright sunlight, what he wanted in those first waking moments was somehow to go back, to find his way into darkness and dreams again.

Orin couldn't remember when he hadn't felt like that. But his father had told him that, like all infants and young children, he'd been a very early riser in those long-ago years. The mornings were noisy with his howls. "Once," his father, Eliot Woodward, had said, "I asked your mother when, for the love of peace and Sunday morning, did children begin to want to sleep in the morning? She said the first day that schools starts. And so it proved to be."

Eliot Woodward also hated to get up in the morning. Victor, Orin's brother, on the other hand, was like their mother. Often, even in the dark and cold of winter, Orin, having finally made the crawl to consciousness, would find Victor awake and dressed, feeding his animals, or reading, or already gone to school. Orin, sitting on the side of his bed, rubbing his eyes, trying to wake up, would wonder how people came to be made the way his mother and brother were. "Freaks," he'd mumble. "Monsters."

For a long time, Orin's mother had taken on the task of getting him up and off to school. They'd had, on school mornings, a contest of wills that left them scarcely speaking to each other by the time he was actually out the door and on his way. Of course, by the time he got home in the afternoon, they'd both forgotten the trouble that morning. And then, unless it was the weekend, the next day would see them locked in the struggle once again.

On Orin's thirteenth birthday, his father had given him a new bike, and his mother had given him a birthday card. She'd written this sentence on it: *My present is that I shall not wake you in the morning anymore.*

Orin had looked at the words in disbelief. Then he glared at his mother, outraged. "How am I supposed to get to school, huh? You know I can't wake up without somebody's help. This isn't fair. I don't want this birthday present. It's the worst one I ever had — anyone ever had."

His mother had lifted her shoulders slightly. "Thirteen year olds must take upon themselves some of the obligations of adulthood. I've spent nearly eight years of school mornings struggling, shouting, and begging to get you moving. I've brought wet washcloths for you to press on your face. I've tickled your feet. I've tried all sorts of measures. I'm finished with them. There are lines on my face that a good night's sleep will never erase, and they are due to you, my dear. I've had it. Up to here."

The next morning, despite an alarm clock and Victor's halfhearted efforts to wake him, Orin slept till nine.

"Now you'll have to write me a note," he snarled.

"A note for what?" asked his mother.

"For being late. You know very well that I've got to take a note saying why I'm tardy. Well, will you write the note for me?"

"Of course." She went into the library, got a sheet of paper and an envelope, came back to the kitchen, wrote a line, folded the paper, put it in the envelope and handed it to him unsealed.

Orin opened it, read the line — *Orin is late because he overslept* — and yelped, "I can't take this to school! And you signed it, *Mommy!* How can I hand in this note at the school office?"

"It's the truth. The people in the office might find it refreshing. I think it's sort of funny."

He dropped into his chair. "Mom, either you write me a proper note —"

"You mean a proper lie?"

"Yes, or I won't go to school. And sign your name. And it isn't funny — anyway, not very."

"Then what do I say in tomorrow's note? Another untruth?"

"You got me into this."

"Orin, you don't really believe that. I won't accept that you believe anything so stupid. It's unworthy of you."

"Look, you don't understand. I don't care if it's worthy or unworthy; that doesn't interest me a bit. I'm just telling you I can't take that — that crazy excuse to school. Maybe I'll drop out. I know how to read and write. I'll educate myself the rest of the way."

"I think you could at that."

They sat together in silence. Orin noticed that his mother's hands were shaking a little as she buttered her toast. So it wasn't all that cut and dried for grownups either, huh? He'd always taken for granted that what they said was what they meant, that how they acted was the way they intended to act. Watching his mother now, he realized that he'd stumbled on a fact he'd just as soon not have known: Grownups aren't always sure of themselves either. Maybe they are unsure in a different way,

or maybe they are unsure in the same way many people his age are unsure. Sometimes grownups say one thing but mean something else. Sometimes they paint themselves into corners with words or actions that they then can't, or won't, go back on. At other times, they blurt out something when it would be better to remain silent. And sometimes, they say nothing when they should speak up. Maybe they don't do this all the time. But here is a fact: His mother was talking in her usual, calm, take-charge voice, but her hands were shaking.

"Why are you upset?" he asked curiously. "You don't have to go to school with a dopey excuse that nobody's going to believe."

"That, Orin, is by no means the most difficult task that is going to be faced by the human race today."

"It's the most difficult one I'm going to face."

"Well, you certainly aren't a man yet."

"Well, I didn't say I was, did I?"

"You'll know that you've taken the first step toward adulthood, or even maturity, when you find yourself faced with a difficulty and can still recognize that it is not the center of the world."

"Suppose it is, I mean, for the person who's having the problem?"

"Oh, no, Orin. Not one person's difficulty or despair or sadness is the central fact of life, any more than his or her happiness is. The sun doesn't go around the world; it's the other way around. And the world isn't tied to you; it's the other way around."

"If you figure that way, in the end you'd have to say that what a person feels doesn't matter at all," argued Orin.

"It matters. It's just not *all* that matters. Oh, well — get me another piece of paper, and I'll write you a lie."

Orin considered. "I guess I'll take this one, after all. It might be sort of interesting to see how the office takes it. Besides, come to think of it, what can they do except bawl me out and tell me to be on time tomorrow? Which," he added, "I won't be, unless somebody agrees to get me up."

162

"You're on your own, Orin."

The woman in the office who received the tardy notes read Orin's, glanced up at him, and smiled. "How original. Go to class, Orin. And don't oversleep except on weekends."

The following morning, probably because he was aware of the 6:45 deadline, Orin managed somehow to wake up and get to school on time. And the next morning, he was on time. But the following, a Friday, he opened his eyes, closed them again, muttered to himself, and went back to sleep.

A little while later, a heavy hand was shaking his shoulder, and his father's voice was loud in his ear. "Orin, get up! Wake up and get out of that bed. *Get up!*"

"Go away," Orin growled, pulling the blanket over his head. "Leave me alone."

The next moment, the blankets and the top sheet were pulled from him, the pillow yanked from underneath his head, and he lay in the cold bedroom, shivering. "At least Mom closes the window when she wakes me up!" he shouted after his father, who yelled back that it was too bad he hadn't known a good thing when he had it.

Twice during the next week, he managed to get himself up, and three times his father stormed in and ripped the bedclothes and pillow away. Orin began to suspect that his father, who also hated to get up in the morning, maybe enjoyed being able to bully someone else awake.

On Saturday, about noontime, Orin came downstairs, yawning noisily. "Okay," he said to his mother. "You win. I'll get myself up from now on. I can't stand being thrashed every school-day morning."

"Oh, Orin — thrashed?"

"When Dad wakes me up, it's like he's hurling thunderbolts around. I think he gets a kick out of it," explained Orin. His mother smiled. Orin yawned again and slumped into the easy chair beside the wood stove.

He couldn't recall how much later after that his mother said one evening, "Orin, I've decided to give you your breakfast in bed."

"Huh? When?"

"On school mornings. I've decided that you can write down what you want for breakfast the evening before, and I'll serve it to you in bed. I'm up anyway, and it might be a more civilized way, a more soothing way, for you to start your day."

Eliot Woodward, who'd been reading, put down his book and said, "Are you serious?"

"Why not?"

"I never heard of anything like it. I've never had my breakfast served to me in bed."

"I'll serve yours, too," she said promptly, "on work mornings."

"You will not, and not his either. Why should you get up early and slave so Orin and I can lie around taking advantage of your kind nature? You're just trying to avoid unpleasantness."

"That's not an unworthy aim. Besides, I'm up early and always get breakfast anyway. I'd quite enjoy fixing trays for you and Orin. You, too, Victor, if you want."

"Nope," Victor said brightly, adding, "I'll help you. That'd be sort of fun. You can carry Orin's tray upstairs, and I'll carry Dad's."

"Good. It's settled. What would you like to eat tomorrow morning, Eliot?"

"I'm getting up for breakfast, and so is Orin."

"Orin isn't, unless he wants to. This is my scheme, not yours. And *I* like the idea."

"Rose, you've had crackpot notions before, but this takes the cake."

"I don't know that it *is* a crackpot notion. After all, we've tried all the usual means of getting a lazy son out of bed on time. We've begged and coaxed and threatened. We've tried force and love and indifference —"

"So we arrive at bribery," remarked Eliot.

"Oh, well, we've arrived someplace. It's worth a try, in my opinion. So, what will you have for breakfast, Orin?"

With his parents' eyes on him, Orin thought about the plan. He decided that in spite of the conflict between his parents, it was still a neat idea.

"I'd like tomato soup and crackers and a little piece of Swiss cheese and a glass of tonic."

"That's breakfast?" Eliot Woodward shouted.

Mrs. Woodward wrote Orin's order on a note pad. "Are you sure you won't change your mind, Eliot?"

"No. I mean yes I'm sure." He glared at Orin and then began to laugh. "I'll be watching with interest to see how long this lasts."

Except for weekends and holidays, it lasted until the time of his mother's fatal car accident. Orin loved having breakfast in bed. All his life, he would remember his mother arriving in the morning with that old tray and some crazy meal, which he'd ordered the night before, arranged prettily just for him. But now, Orin knew, nothing quite so nice as that would ever happen to him again.

THE MEAT MARKET MYSTERY

by Margaret P. Strachan

Kathy Ruiz paused outside Skinner's Market, going over in her mind what had just happened. She needed a job, but Mr. Skinner had said he didn't need any more workers, even though his store was the busiest one in town. Slowly, she walked down the street.

Joe Menendez, Kathy's boyfriend, was stacking boxes behind the other big market in town. A single car stood in the parking lot. Kathy tried to look as if she weren't disappointed about not getting the job, but Joe understood.

"Mr. Glenn's wife is in the hospital. Maybe you can work here with me tonight."

Inside the market, a few shoppers pushed carts along the aisles. A single checker rang up the groceries. Joe stopped at the meat counter where Mr. Glenn held out a beef roast for a customer.

"I know the price per pound is high," Mr. Glenn was saying, "but it's prime beef."

"Mr. Skinner has prime beef too," the customer replied.

"I can't sell at his prices."

"I'm sorry, Mr. Glenn."

Kathy thought this was a poor time to ask for a job, but Joe spoke up quickly. Mr. Glenn slowly put the roast back in the case. He studied Kathy's face a minute before he answered.

"You can help Joe tonight," he said, "by staying until I return from the hospital."

"*¡Gracias!*" Kathy said. "Thanks!" Getting paid for a few hours of work was better than nothing.

This was the first winter the Ruiz family had stayed in the Pacific Northwest after the picking season had ended. Usually they returned to Texas. But Kathy's father had found a job at the lumberyard. A long-lasting job instead of one as a migrant worker was her father's dream. And her mother longed to have a home in the same place so Kathy and her brothers and sisters wouldn't have to change schools several times a year.

Joe gave Kathy a bucket and showed her how to wash the windows so that the plate glass would not streak. Looking over at Skinner's Market, Kathy could see people leaving, loaded down with bags. At closing time, she saw the checkers and butchers leave. She thought of the customer who said Mr. Skinner's meat was cheaper. How could Mr. Skinner sell meat for less than Mr. Glenn?

The sharp ring of the telephone interrupted Kathy's thoughts. Mr. Glenn had gone. Joe was busy scrubbing a counter. "You get it," he said. "It's probably a wrong number."

Kathy hurried to Mr. Glenn's tiny office.

"Mr. Glenn," a man's voice said, "I know you, see. You don't know me. I have something to offer you, see."

Kathy began, "Mr. Glenn has gone . . . ," but the voice kept on.

"It's like this, see. I've got cheap beef for sale. Get smart before you go broke! I'll be in your neighborhood tonight, see. What do you say?"

"Mr. Glenn is not here. Do you want to leave a number?"

"WHAT?" The receiver clicked. Kathy stared at the telephone. The line was dead.

Kathy rushed out to Joe. "Some guy said he sold cheap beef. When he found out that I wasn't Mr. Glenn, he hung up!"

"You're kidding," said Joe.

"*Seriamente.* No fooling," Kathy said. "He said he had something to offer. He said Mr. Glenn should get smart before he goes broke!"

"Someone is selling meat illegally!"

"That is how Mr. Skinner . . ." Joe and Kathy stared at each other, eyes wide. "Joe," Kathy added, "he said he'd be in the neighborhood tonight."

"We'll tell Mr. Glenn," Joe said.

But when the store owner returned, he refused to listen.

"You watch too many TV mysteries. Meat is checked by the government and stamped. You didn't understand, or someone is trying to tease me. Everyone knows I'm losing my shirt." Mr. Glenn ran his fingers through his hair and shook his head. "The way my wife looked, I'll have to spend tomorrow evening at the hospital too. Kathy, you've worked hard and done a good job. Come back tomorrow with Joe."

"*Gracias,* Mr. Glenn. I've worked in the fields picking strawberries and beans. This work is easier!"

"But, Mr. Glenn," Joe said, "don't you think maybe Mr. Skinner . . ."

"Forget it!" Mr. Glenn said. "I'm no pal of his, but his meat has to be stamped just like mine!"

Outside, the shops were dimly lighted. Suddenly, Kathy grabbed Joe's arm.

"Look in Skinner's lot."

A stream of light from the rear delivery door showed a parked truck.

"That could belong to the man who was on the phone. Should we call the police?" Kathy whispered.

Joe shook his head. "They wouldn't believe us any more than Mr. Glenn did."

There was no traffic. After pausing for a few minutes, the two ran across the street to look into Skinner's front window. No one was in sight. They slipped around the corner of the building but ducked back when they heard a man's voice.

"That's all until tomorrow, see. You can be glad there is that much!"

"Don't get excited. Come in for some coffee. But wait until I wash off the pavement. You sure leave a trail of blood," Mr. Skinner said.

"What do you expect," asked the man, "refrigerated deliveries? That beef was on the hoof a few hours ago!"

There was the sound of water hitting the pavement. Then the door slammed, and the stream of light disappeared. Kathy breathed out slowly.

"That was the guy! He said 'see' the same way," said Kathy. "Let's find the name on that truck."

"Your mom is going to be mad if you're late getting home," Joe reminded her.

"We'll hurry," she answered Joe.

But there was no name on the truck. Joe tried the back

door, but it was locked. Kathy bent down to read the license-plate number.

"That truck comes from east of the mountains," Joe said. "Rustlers! There were stories in the paper about them. Some farmers have banded together to police the roads."

"Mr. Skinner must have a hidden stamp that he uses!" Kathy said.

"Mr. Skinner stamps the meat himself!" Joe exclaimed. "Wow! What a crooked deal!"

"*¡Tranquilo!* Quiet!" whispered Kathy.

The delivery door was opening. Joe caught Kathy's hand, and the pair ran around the building. They moved into the dark shadow of the brick wall.

"I'll be here the same time tomorrow," the driver said. "Don't forget my signal — three raps, a pause, and then three more."

"Quit worrying," Mr. Skinner said.

"You'd worry, too, if you carried hot meat over the mountains. After I make enough money, I'll drop this business."

The truck started. Kathy poked Joe. They dropped to the pavement so they couldn't be seen. The truck pulled out of the lot and swung left. Its faint taillights disappeared down the street.

Kathy tried to hear Mr. Skinner returning to the store. She feared he might discover them. But the rear door shut softly.

"Tomorrow," Joe said, "after Mr. Glenn leaves, you go to the police."

"*Me?* I've never talked to an officer before."

"Officers don't bite," said Joe. "Staying at the store is my job."

"Okay," said Kathy. "But the police won't pay any attention to me!" If only Mr. Glenn had understood!

The next afternoon when it was nearly closing time, Kathy and Joe tried to get Mr. Glenn to speak to the police. But he wanted to leave for the hospital at once.

"This may be my last week," he said, "but I want a clean place."

"Are things that bad?" asked Joe.

"I can't even sell this store for enough money to pay the doctor and hospital bills!" Mr. Glenn said.

As Kathy straightened the shelves of canned goods, she tried to plan what she'd say at the police station. Going to the police took a lot of courage. She found it hard to collect her thoughts. At last, it was time to leave.

When Kathy reached the police station, she was greeted by a uniformed officer.

"Joe Menendez and I," Kathy gulped, "we . . . we work for Glenn's Market. We . . . we saw . . . "

"Saw what?" asked the officer.

In a rush, words tumbling over each other, Kathy told her everything.

"Come and tell the chief your story," the officer said.

To Kathy's surprise, the chief was as courteous to Kathy as he would have been to an adult. Encouraged, she told the chief what she and Joe had seen and heard.

"Kathy," the chief said, "we need more evidence before we can go to court and get a search warrant. Then a judge will decide whether or not we can act. Will you swear to what you've seen and heard? Will your parents let you?"

"I think they will," said Kathy hopefully.

The chief called out, "Sal, did you hear that? Check with Kathy's parents and with the Menendez family. We'll need both Joe and Kathy to go before the judge."

Kathy knew the police chief expected her to go home as soon as Mr. Glenn returned that evening. But she and Joe couldn't resist hiding behind the Goodwill box near Skinner's Market. The lot was like a big, dark cave. A cold wind sent shivers up Kathy's back.

Joe whispered, "We should see the police soon! Man! It must be exciting to catch crooks. Maybe I could go to college and study —"

Joe broke off. Kathy saw his face in the dim light from a distant streetlamp. His eyes shone.

"Joe, I'd like to become an officer too. The police would take a Chicana if her marks were good. *¿Quién sabe?*"

They hushed then, waiting for the sound of the truck. A single car drove by, rounded the corner, and was gone. No late shoppers walked the street, and the only sound was the distant hum of the freeway traffic.

"Joe," Kathy whispered, "what if the guy doesn't come?"

"He'll come! But I guess the police didn't bother."

At last, a truck rumbled down the street. The driver climbed out, went to Skinner's rear door, and knocked — three raps, a long pause, then three more raps. Kathy's eyes burned as she tried to see across the way. Mr. Skinner opened the door, and the two men went to the truck. Both went inside it, then came hurrying out with huge objects that Kathy knew were sides of beef.

There was a long period of no activity. Then the driver came out and went to his truck. He called back over his shoulder. "No coffee tonight. There is snow on the pass. I'll have to put on chains." He climbed into the cab of the truck but leaned out to finish speaking. "Your end is easy. Keep that stamp hidden. If anyone spots it, we'll all serve time!"

"Don't worry. It's locked in my safe," Mr. Skinner said.

"I'd feel better if Glenn were buying. One night he just may be around here!" said the driver.

"He'd never go for it. You were lucky that he wasn't in when you phoned. He'll be out of business any day now."

Mr. Skinner's voice faded as the truck motor roared. Kathy and Joe stayed huddled behind the Goodwill box until they heard the door slam. Kathy was disappointed.

"The police didn't believe me," she said. "Probably the chief went to Mr. Skinner and gave the show away."

"Si." Joe broke into Spanish. "¡No importa! No matter. You tried."

Joe pulled up Kathy. She was stiff from kneeling. He caught her hand, and they started up the street. Anger replaced her disappointment.

"I must not be very smart if I couldn't get the police to believe me. Joe, do you think Mr. Skinner paid off the police?"

"Now you sound as if you've seen too many TV mysteries," Joe answered.

"Well, why weren't the police there?" asked Kathy.

"I suppose you wish we'd gone into Skinner's Market to look for the stamp? Maybe you think I could open the safe?"

Kathy smiled. She did wish that.

The soft purring of a car motor crept up on them. Kathy looked back. This was the darkest part of her block. As the car edged toward the curb, she couldn't help but shiver. Someone meant to speak to them.

"Kathy?" a woman's voice questioned. "Joe?"

Kathy was relieved when she recognized the officer named Sal. She and another officer were in an unmarked car. Suddenly, Kathy remembered that this was the car that she had seen earlier. Kathy and Joe moved to the curb.

"You two did a good job," Sal said. "We talked with your parents, and you're to be in court tomorrow. Then we'll search Skinner's Market."

"Did you hear him say that the stamp was in the safe?" Joe asked.

Sal laughed. "You didn't miss much. I saw you kneeling behind the Goodwill box. I'm glad you stayed hidden. A lot of police work is sitting and waiting. It can be mighty dull. But even when you're sure someone is guilty, you have to go through the due process of law. The police enter a place only after they have gotten a search warrant."

"We . . . we thought you didn't come," Kathy admitted.

"We were there, all right," Sal said. "Now what can I say but *gracias* and *buenas noches?*" With a friendly wave, the officers drove away.

"Mr. Glenn's business will pick up now," Joe said.

"And," Kathy added, "someone else will have Skinner's Market. Then maybe I can get a steady job there! *¡Muy bien!*"

Survival Skill
Reading Transportation Schedules

Intown Bus Schedule

Almost every city has buses that carry riders from one part of the city to another. Some cities include bus service for the nearby towns as well. Each bus follows a particular route. A bus travels along this route according to a schedule. So that the passengers will know when to expect a bus, the bus company has a printed schedule. The schedule tells the times that a bus leaves from and arrives at a bus stop.

Most intown bus schedules look something like the one on the next page. Notice that there are two parts to it. The left side gives the times a bus leaves Heights Park to go downtown; the right side lists the times a bus leaves downtown to go to Heights Park. Read the titles of the three columns that are on each side. Usually there is different service during the week than on weekends. On weekdays, buses run more often because people use them to get to work and to school. On Saturdays, people may take buses to go to work or to do shopping. Sunday is the least busy day.

To understand an intown bus schedule, you must know how to read it. Read down the first WEEKDAY column on the left side, HEIGHTS PARK TO DOWNTOWN. Do you see that right under 6:45 A.M., it says "Ev. 30 min."? That means there is a bus leaving Heights Park for downtown every thirty minutes between 6:45 A.M. and 9:15 A.M. After 9:15 A.M., how often does a bus leave for downtown? Yes, there is a bus every hour until 4:15 P.M. A bus leaves at 10:15 and 11:15 A.M. and at 12:15, 1:15, 2:15, and 3:15 P.M. On the schedule, A.M. or P.M. appears only beside the first listed hour for that time of day.

HEIGHTS PARK TO DOWNTOWN			DOWNTOWN TO HEIGHTS PARK		
WEEKDAY	SATURDAY	SUNDAY	WEEKDAY	SATURDAY	SUNDAY
6:45 AM	6:20 AM	9:30 AM	7:20 AM	8:15 AM	8:30 AM
Ev. 30 min.	7:20	Hourly	8:15	Ev. 30 min.	Hourly
9:15	X 8:15	11:30 PM	Hourly	5:15 PM	11:30 PM
Hourly	Ev. 30 min.	12:15 AM	4:15 PM	Hourly	
4:15 PM	5:15 PM		4:50	12:15 AM	
5:20	Hourly		X 5:15		
6:15	12:15 AM		5:30		
Hourly			6:00		
12:15 AM			Hourly		
			12:15 AM		

Running time: 56 minutes	Express running time: 45 minutes	X: Express

Now read the SATURDAY column for HEIGHTS PARK TO DOWNTOWN. Notice that there is an X in front of 8:15. Read the words at the bottom of the schedule. They tell you that X stands for "Express." An express bus does not stop to pick up riders or let them off once it has left the station. Usually, an express bus gets you to your destination faster than a bus that makes several stops. What is the running time for the express bus? Yes, it usually takes the express bus only 45 minutes to go from Heights Park to downtown or downtown to Heights Park. A bus that is not an express takes 56 minutes to go from Heights Park to downtown or downtown to Heights Park.

Commuter Train Schedule

Look at the commuter train schedule on the next page. This schedule tells you the times that a train leaves Carver and the times it stops in several towns before arriving at Wells City. When the train stops at Ingles, Reedsville, and Greenton, it lets off and picks up passengers. When does the first train leave Reedsville? The

LEAVE:				ARRIVE:
Carver	Ingles	Reedsville	Greenton	Wells City
* 7:03	* 7:08	* 7:13	* 7:16	* 7:40
7:44	7:49	7:54	7:57	8:20
8:44	. . . .	. . . .	. . . .	9:10
9:48	9:53	9:58	10:01	10:24
1:48	1:53	. . . .	2:01	2:20
3:48	3:53	3:58	4:01	4:24
* 5:02	* 5:07	* 5:14	* 5:17	* 5:42
5:42	5:47	5:54	5:58	6:23
8:42	8:47	8:52	8:55	9:18

. . . . Train does not stop to let off or pick up passengers.

Lightface — A.M.

Boldface — P.M.

* Does not run Saturday and Sunday.

first train leaves at 7:13 A.M. At the bottom of the schedule, you can see that the lightfaced type means "A.M." and that the boldfaced type means "P.M." Look at the first time a train leaves Carver. Do you see the symbol before the time, 7:03? The * shows that a train does not leave Carver at that time on Saturday and Sunday. When does the first train leave Carver on Saturday and Sunday? That's right, at 7:44 A.M. Notice that in some columns, instead of a time listed, there are four dots. What do these dots stand for? Look again at the bottom of the schedule. The dots indicate that the train does not stop to let off or pick up passengers. Because the 8:44 A.M. train for Carver does not stop in Ingles, Reedsville, and Greenton, it takes less time to reach Wells City than the 7:44 A.M. train.

Long Distance Bus Schedule

On the next page is a long distance bus schedule. When you read down the three narrow columns on the left, the schedule is for bus service from Chicago, Illinois, to the last city listed, Los Angeles, California.

Read Down					Read Up		
310	320	301	SCHEDULE NUMBERS		342	361	345
8:15	**4:00**	2:00	Lv Chicago, Ill. (CT)	Ar	5:00	7:15	**7:05**
4:00	**12:20**	10:00	Lv Des Moines, Ia. (CT)	Ar	**8:50**	12:01	8:50
7:35	**4:15**	**2:30**	Lv Omaha, Nebr. (CT)	Ar	**4:15**	**8:10**	4:45
7:00	**3:25**	**1:30**	Ar Cheyenne, Wyo. (MT)	Lv	**3:15**	**7:20**	**4:45**
8:00	**4:45**	**3:00**	Lv Cheyenne, Wyo. (MT)	Ar	**2:20**	**6:10**	**3:40**
5:05	1:55	**1:25**	Ar Salt Lake City, Utah (MT)	Lv	**4:30**	**9:05**	6:00
6:40	**3:00**	**2:30**	Lv Salt Lake City, Utah (MT)	Ar	**2:45**	**6:50**	**4:10**
4:15	11:35	**11:00**	Ar Las Vegas, Nev. (PT)	Lv	**3:10**	**7:20**	**5:30**
5:00	**12:15**	**11:45**	Lv Las Vegas, Nev. (PT)	Ar	**2:35**	**6:30**	**4:35**
11:25	**5:55**	6:00	Ar Los Angeles, Calif. (PT)	Lv	**7:30**	12:15	9:45

(CT) — Central Time	Lightface — A.M.	Ar — Arrive
(MT) — Mountain Time	**Boldface — P.M.**	Lv — Leave
(PT) — Pacific Time		

When you read up the three narrow columns on the right, the schedule is for bus service from Los Angeles to Chicago. The center column lists the cities along the route where the bus stops. At some cities, the bus stops just to let off passengers and pick up others. Those cities — Des Moines, Iowa, and Omaha, Nebraska — are just listed once. At the other cities, the bus stops long enough for passengers to get off, stretch their legs, make a phone call, or get something to eat. Those cities are listed twice. The time is given when the bus arrives at the station and when it leaves. At the bottom of the schedule, the abbreviations "Ar" and "Lv" are explained. Also at the bottom of the schedule, you see that lightfaced type indicates "A.M." and that boldfaced type indicates "P.M."

Now read down the first column, schedule number 310. Would you have time to get a snack when you got to Cheyenne, Wyoming? Yes, you would. How can you tell? Yes, the schedule says that you arrive at 7:00 P.M. and leave at 8:00 P.M. You are in Cheyenne for an hour.

Notice that beside the name of each city and state the abbreviation for the time zone is given. The time zones and abbreviations are listed at the bottom of the schedule. On your trip west — from Chicago to Los Angeles — you would set your watch *back* one hour for each time zone. So, you would set your watch *back* twice. On your trip east — from Los Angeles to Chicago — you would set your watch *ahead* one hour for each time zone. So, you would set your watch *ahead* twice. The time changes have already been figured on the schedule.

Now let's say that you are going from Los Angeles to Des Moines, Iowa. Look at schedule number 345 and read up. You would leave Los Angeles at 9:45 A.M. on Tuesday. Where would you be at that time on Wednesday? You would be somewhere between Salt Lake City, Utah, and Cheyenne, Wyoming. When would you arrive in Des Moines, Iowa? You would arrive at the bus station in Des Moines at 8:50 A.M. on Thursday. Your trip would take you almost two days.

Now use the intown bus schedule, the commuter train schedule, and the long distance bus schedule to answer each of the following questions. Use a separate piece of paper. Write the number of each question and the letter of the correct answer.

1. Martha lives in Heights Park and works downtown on Monday through Friday. She must be at work at 9:00 A.M. The bus stop is a five-minute walk from her office. What is the last bus she can take to get to work on time?
    a. 7:15 A.M.   c. 8:15 A.M.
    b. 7:45 A.M.   d. 8:00 A.M.

2. Jim and Sunny live downtown and want to go to Heights Park for a picnic on Sunday. They would like to get to Heights Park a little before noon and arrive home by 7:00 P.M. Which two buses should they take?
    a. 11:30 A.M. to Heights Park; 5:30 P.M. to downtown
    b. 9:30 A.M. to Heights Park; 6:30 P.M. to downtown
    c. 10:30 A.M. to Heights Park; 6:30 P.M. to downtown
    d. 10:30 A.M. to Heights Park; 5:30 P.M. to downtown

3. Sam lives in Heights Park. On Saturday, he wants to go shopping downtown. He'd like to get there just as the stores open at 9:00 A.M. Which bus should be take?
    a. 8:15 A.M. (express)   c. 8:45 A.M.
    b. 7:20 A.M.   d. 8:00 A.M.

4. Jerome lives in Ingles. He has to be at work in Wells City every morning at 9:30 A.M. The train station is a ten-minute walk from his office. What time should he take the train to arrive at work on time?
    a. 8:44 A.M.   c. 7:54 A.M.
    b. 7:49 A.M.   d. 7:44 A.M.

5. Marsha lives in Carver and wants to visit her friend Janet in Reedsville. Which of the following trains would *not* take her to Reedsville?
    a. 9:48 A.M.   c. 8:42 P.M.
    b. 3:48 P.M.   d. 1:48 P.M.

6. Cary and Jamie want to get to Los Angeles around 6:00 P.M. on Sunday. On which day must they leave by bus from Chicago?
    a. Saturday   c. Thursday
    b. Friday   d. Sunday

7. At which cities should Cary and Jamie set their watches back one hour when going by bus from Chicago to Los Angeles?
    a. Des Moines, la. and Las Vegas, Nev.
    b. Salt Lake City, Utah and Los Angeles, Calif.
    c. Cheyenne, Wyo. and Las Vegas, Nev.
    d. Salt Lake City, Utah and Los Angeles, Calif.

8. Marc is taking a bus from Los Angeles with the schedule number 361. At Salt Lake City, Utah, he wants to catch a bus to Portland, Oregon. The bus for Portland leaves Salt Lake City at 7:30 P.M. Will Marc arrive in Salt Lake City in time to catch the bus to Portland?
    a. Yes   c. You can't tell from the
    b. No   schedule.

One Hundred Years of Peace, ALMOST

by Charlotte Pomerantz

This fable of an ancient time was suggested by an incident involving Vietnam and the Imperial Navy of Kublai Khan, in the thirteenth century.

A very long time ago, there was a small patch of dry land called the Tiny Kingdom. Most of its people were poor farmers or fisherfolk. Their bodies were lean and brown and strong from working long hours in the sun. They built the thatched mud huts in which they lived. They wove the simple earth-colored clothing they wore. And everyone, even the children, helped to plow the fields, harvest the rice, and catch the fish that they ate.

The land of the Tiny Kingdom was as poor as its people. The soil had neither gold nor silver, which

Adapted from *The Princess and the Admiral,* © 1974, by Charlotte Pomerantz, a Young Scott Book, by permission of Addison-Wesley Publishing Company, Inc.

was why no country, in the memory of the oldest man or woman, had ever made war against them. The people were good-humored about the poverty of the land. It had given them a hundred years of peace.

The ruler of the Tiny Kingdom was Mat Mat, a dark-eyed young princess. One night, almost a thousand years ago, the Princess looked out the window of her royal bedchamber at the fishing boats in the harbor below, then up at the pale sliver of a moon.

Tonight, the young Princess was too excited to sleep, for this month marked One Hundred Years of Peace in the Tiny Kingdom. It would be celebrated, as were all great events, with a Carnival and Fireworks Display. Tomorrow morning, at the Council of Three Advisers, the Princess would choose the date.

There would be all kinds of firecrackers — flares, rockets, and pinwheels that burst into flowers and waterfalls and fishes. Birds and butterflies would fly among trees of green fire. Then, at midnight, one — no, three — red dragons would glide across the night sky.

"Beautiful!" murmured the Princess, her dark eyes shining.

The next morning, the Princess was the first to arrive at the Council Chamber. The three advisers followed: first, the Elder, a man of

ninety years, then, the Younger, a man of eighty years, and finally, In-Between, who was exactly eighty-five.

The Princess greeted them. "Joyful tidings, my dear advisers. This month marks One Hundred Years of Peace in the Tiny Kingdom. I think you will agree that this calls for a very special Carnival and Fireworks Display."

The three advisers were strangely silent and stone-faced.

The Elder broke the silence. "Excuse me, Your Highness, but there can be no celebration."

"Why not?" asked the Princess.

"There are stories about an invasion," said the Younger.

"It looks like war," said In-Between.

The Princess stared at them, unbelieving. "But we have no enemies."

"I fear we do," said the Elder. "We have just had a report from our fishing boats that a large fleet of warships is now sailing toward our kingdom."

"How terrible!" said the Princess. "How many ships are coming?"

"Our fishing boats report twenty ships of war," said In-Between, "including the flagship of the Admiral."

"How large are the ships?"

"I would judge each to be about five times the size of the Royal Swan Boat," said the Elder.

"More like four times the size of the largest fishing boat," said the Younger.

"Mmm," said In-Between. "I'd say the truth lies somewhere in the middle."

"Never mind," said the Princess impatiently. "How long will it be before the enemy fleet reaches the harbor of the Tiny Kingdom?"

"Two days, more or less," the advisers replied in chorus.

The Princess walked to the window and looked at the harbor below. "We have no forts, no soldiers, no weapons, no ships of war," she mused. "Clearly, we shall have to rely on . . . other things." She walked briskly back to the throne. "Call in the Court Astrologer," she said.

The three advisers shrugged. "With all due respect," said the Younger, "astrology cannot be used in place of weapons."

"We'll see," said the Princess.

An old woman tottered into the Council Chamber.

"Your Highness wants me?" she asked.

"I seek information about the position of the sun and the moon," said the Princess.

"With pleasure," said the old woman. "When the moon is in its first or third quarter, it's as if it were a stranger to the sun. But when it is a new moon or a full moon, there is a special, rather remarkable attraction. We see it in

plants and oceans on Earth. I often feel it in my bones."

"And what of the moon tonight?"

"Tonight it is a new moon that hangs its bright lantern over your Tiny Kingdom."

"Interesting," said the Princess. "You may return to your tower."

The Princess beckoned her three advisers to come close. "Our course is clear," she said, "as clear as the lantern moon." The four of them huddled together while the Princess whispered her plan.

"And so," she said, "the first order of business is to send out a dozen of our fishing boats to tease the enemy. Their ships are bound to chase ours, and if everything goes well, the enemy ships should get here at the right time."

The next day, upon orders of Princess Mat Mat, hundreds of farmers, fisherfolk, and children gathered in a nearby forest to cut down the tallest trees. The strongest men and women sawed through the trunks. The least strong sharpened both ends of the fallen trees, and the children stripped off the branches.

Then everyone helped to haul the tree poles to the riverbed. When the tide had gone down enough for the people to drag the poles into the water, they hammered them — dozens and dozens of them — into the muddy bottom of the riverbed.

The Princess watched from the window of her royal bedchamber. When she had counted 253 poles, sticking out of the water like a crazy, uneven picket fence, she gave orders for the people to return to their huts.

The next morning, when the Princess and her advisers stood on the Royal Balcony, not a single pole could be seen.

"I thought the tide would be higher," said the Elder.

"I thought it would be lower," said the Younger.

"Your Highness," said In-Between, "I think you guessed just right."

"It was no guess," said the Princess. "Not after I talked to the Court Astrologer. We know the tides are caused by the attraction of the sun and the moon. Therefore, when I learned that these two bodies are closer at this time, I knew that the tide would be extra high — high enough to cover the tree poles." The Princess smiled. "The moon is a faithful friend."

Just then, the first ships of the enemy fleet were sighted nearing the mouth of the riverbed. They were in full chase of the twelve fishing boats that had been sent out to tease them.

The enemy ships sailed up the middle of the river. As they faced the village, fifty more fishing boats appeared from all directions and surrounded them.

Aboard the flagship of the enemy fleet, the Admiral ordered, "Furl sails and drop anchor! Get ready to fight!"

From the Royal Balcony, the Princess looked down at the enemy ships and clapped her hands.

"He did it! The Admiral did just what I hoped he would do!" she exclaimed, trying hard not to jump up and down.

On the river, the Admiral peered uneasily at all the fishing boats. "It looks as if the fisherfolk are going to climb aboard."

"But, sir," said the Captain, "they don't seem to have any weapons."

As he spoke, the fisherfolk began to hurl cooking pots, soup ladles, coconuts, fruits, chickens — whatever they had been able to get hold of — at the enemy fleet. One of the fisherfolk took a whole pail of eels and threw it aboard the Admiral's flagship. Then the little fishing boats turned round and quickly sailed past the harbor, leaving the Admiral and his warships in full command of the river.

The Admiral was delighted. "Did those people really think they could conquer our mighty fleet with coconuts and cooking pots?"

"It would seem that they are a rather primitive people, sir," said the Captain.

The Admiral looked over the village and the castle. "No trouble here," he said smugly. "The fishing boats have disappeared behind a bend in the river. There is not a living thing on the streets, except for a few chickens and goats. It's clear the people are terrified." He looked down at the water. "The tide is going out, but there's still plenty of depth here in the middle of the river. We'll wait for low tide to make sure we can dock."

Settling comfortably into his deck chair, he said, "Tomorrow, first thing, we'll surround the palace, search for and destroy the weapons, seize the crown jewels, and behead the Princess."

"An hour later, as the Admiral was napping in his deck chair, a loud shout came from below deck. "Shipping water!"

"What's that supposed to mean?" barked the Admiral.

"It means there's a leak," said the Captain.

From all over the fleet came the cry, "Shipping water! We're shipping water!"

The Admiral dashed down to the hold. There, an unbelievable sight greeted his eyes. What appeared to be the top of a tree was poking through the bottom of the ship! Even as the Admiral watched, the treetop was slowly coming upward — then another tree . . . and another . . . and another. More than a dozen treetops were coming through the bottom! And where the wood had split

around the tree trunks, the water was beginning to seep in, slowly but steadily.

"Start bailing and saw off those crazy trees," yelled the Admiral.

"Beg pardon, sir," said the Captain, "but if you get rid of the trees, the water will rush through. The trees are like plugs. Take away the plugs, and we will all drown in the onrushing waters."

"Never mind," said the Admiral crossly. "Send a message to the fleet: All ships to continue bailing."

Some two hours later, the Captain stuck his head in the cabin door. "Sorry to bother you, sir, but the water is draining out of the ships."

"Naturally, you blockhead," said the Admiral. "All hands are bailing."

"No, no," said the Captain. "It's happening all by itself."

"I'd better have a look!" gasped the Admiral.

He strode out on deck, stumbled on a coconut, then stopped and stared goggle-eyed at the amazing sight. All around, his whole fleet was stuck up on tree poles! The air resounded with loud crackings and bangings coming from the bottoms of all the ships as they settled firmly onto the tree trunks. And, of course, the seawater was drip-dripping out of the bottoms of all the raised ships.

Suddenly everything became

clear to the Admiral. He had been trapped. These clever fisherfolk had used the tide against him. They had put in poles at low tide. He had come in with his ships at high tide. Then, when the tide went out, the ships were left stuck up on the poles.

Now he could hear the roar of laughter from the farmers, fisherfolk, and children who crowded the riverbank and docks.

From around the bend, the little fishing boats reappeared and surrounded the fleet. At their head was the Royal Swan Boat, flying a flag of peace under the royal standard. It sailed up alongside the Admiral's flagship.

"Ahoy, mate," said a tall member of the fisherfolk. "Are you ready to give up?"

The Admiral looked down and shook his fist. "Never! You just wait till we come ashore."

The tall man grinned. "If you're thinking of sending your people swimming or wading to shore, think again. Because any person found in the water will be whacked on the head with an oar."

"Who are you?" thundered the Admiral.

"I'm the best of the fisherfolk around. Because I sacrificed a whole pail of eels for the glory of the Tiny Kingdom, the Princess has given me the honor of taking you to shore to talk over the terms of peace."

"Never!" said the Admiral. "I will go down with my ship."

"Your ship isn't going to go down," said the tall man. "It will stay stuck up there on the tree poles until the tides break the whole fleet apart."

The Admiral sighed, climbed down, and settled gloomily in the Royal Swan Boat. The tall man rowed him to shore.

After the Admiral had changed into dry socks, he was called to the Council Chamber to face Princess Mat Mat and her three advisers.

The Princess led the Admiral to the window overlooking the harbor.

"It's a beautiful sight, isn't it?" she said.

The Admiral turned red. "Beautiful! It's a nightmare."

"Try to get hold of yourself," said the Princess.

"What a loss of pride!" cried the Admiral. "To be defeated by a woman!" He glanced at the young princess. "Not even a woman. A slip of a girl." His shoulders dropped. "What's the difference? I shall be beheaded at dawn."

"Certainly, we will behead you," said the Elder.

"I would cut off his feet," said the Younger.

"In my opinion," said In-Between, "justice lies somewhere in the middle."

The Princess clucked her tongue in disapproval. "Are you such old men that you have forgotten the story of the widow and her chickens?"

"Your Highness," said the Elder, "every child in this kingdom knows it by heart."

"Perhaps it is time to tell it again," said the Princess. She faced them all and began her tale.

"*Once upon a time, there was a poor old widow who saw a young man sneak into her yard and steal two chickens. She knew very well who the young man was, but she did not report him to the authorities. Instead, that evening, when everyone, including the young man, had gathered in the village square to watch the Carnival and Fireworks Display, the widow called out, 'What kind of person steals two chickens from a poor old woman? I'll tell you — a no-good thief with a heart of stone. Shame on this person. Shame! Shame!'*

"*The young man listened and was indeed ashamed. That very night, he sneaked into the widow's yard and returned one of the chickens. (He had, alas, cooked and eaten the other one.) The widow saw him and hid. 'It is good,' she said. 'I got back one of my chickens, and the young man did not lose face in the village.'"*

When the Princess had finished her tale, she turned to the Admiral and said, "So you see, sir, revenge is not our way. We do not believe that those who have wronged us should be punished or lose face beyond what is necessary."

"You are not going to behead me?" said the Admiral.

"Ugh," said the Princess. "How distasteful."

The Admiral was completely confused. "Your Highness, what are you going to do?"

"Simple," said the Princess. "I shall supply you with two guides to take you and your warriors through the harsh mountains that lead back to your country and your Emperor. I shall also provide you with a two-week supply of food and water, as well as five water buffaloes to help carry your goods." The Princess was thoughtful. "Of course, we would like you to return the water buffaloes."

The Admiral knelt down before the Princess and kissed her hand. "Be assured, your animals shall be returned." His voice trembled with thanks and relief. "Your Highness, I shall never forget you nor the kind and gentle ways of your kingdom." Tears filled his eyes, rolled down his cheeks and onto his gold medals. "If there is anything I can ever do for you . . ."

"As a matter of fact, there is," said the Princess.

"Anything," repeated the Admiral.

The Princess eyed him coolly

and said, "I would ask you not to make unkind remarks about women and girls — especially princesses."

That evening, from the Royal Balcony, Princess Mat Mat and her three advisers watched the long winding line of enemy soldiers and sailors. The water buffaloes pulled carts heavily-laden with food and water. At the front, leading his warriors, the Admiral, bedecked with medals and sniffling from a head cold, sat astride the fattest water buffalo. All along the road winding into the mountains, the farmers, fisherfolk, and children waved them good-bye.

"It is good," said the Princess to her advisers. "We won the battle, and since the Admiral is returning home with all his warriors, he will not lose too much face with his Emperor." She sighed longingly. "How close we came to celebrating One Hundred Years of Peace."

"Dear Princess," said the Elder, "what happened this morning could hardly be called a battle. The only casualty was a sailor who got bonged on the head with a cooking pot."

"It was more like a small fight," said the Younger. "But I thought the sailor got bonged on the toe."

"That's odd," said In-Between. "I was sure it was a coconut."

"My dear advisers," said the Princess, "do I understand you to mean that we can go ahead with the plans for the celebration?"

The Elder shrugged. "If the poor widow could forget about one of her chickens, surely we can forget one small event in a hundred years of peace."

"For the first time," said the Younger, "the three of us are in agreement about the number of firecrackers, flares, torches, Bengal lights, rockets, Roman candles, and pinwheels for the celebration — one thousand."

The Princess was overjoyed. "Why that's more than I ever dreamed of! And will there be three dragons?"

"About the dragons," said the Elder, "we don't think three is the right number."

"Oh, my," said the Princess. "How many, then?"

"We shall see," said In-Between.

So it came to pass that within the week, the Tiny Kingdom celebrated One Hundred Years of Peace — well, almost — with the biggest Carnival and Fireworks Display in its history. Not one, not three, but *twelve* red dragons glided across the night sky.

And of all the happy farmers, fisherfolk, and children in the Tiny Kingdom, not one was happier than Princess Mat Mat.

Augusta Savage

**by Romare Bearden
and Harry Henderson**

One day in 1906, a six-year-old black girl was playing with some red clay that was found everywhere in Green Cove Springs, Florida. This little girl made a discovery. She rolled that sticky clay into a ball. Then she narrowed it and turned up one end to make a point. By squeezing another piece of clay into a long neck and sticking it onto the ball, she made a duck. And she discovered that if she tried harder, she could make it look like a real duck — with its neck gracefully curved and head tucked down or stuck straight out with wings spread.

Although Augusta Savage did not know it then, she had started something she could not stop: making things with her hands in clay, in stone, and sometimes in wood. Shaping things with her strong hands was an act that was always deeply interesting and pleasing to her.

Augusta was the seventh child of fourteen children born to a minister and his wife. The family was poor. There were few toys and playthings. Perhaps this was why Augusta made the duck. Every chance Augusta got, she would go to the clay pits to model ducks, animals, and human figures.

When Augusta was fifteen years old, her family moved to West Palm Beach. Although she looked in many places, she could find no clay there.

Then one day, she was riding in the school wagon with the principal, Professor Mickens. Augusta saw a small factory, the Chase Pottery. Instantly the desire to model something in clay overcame her. She leaped from the wagon and disappeared into the clay factory. When Professor Mickens came in a few minutes later, he saw Augusta begging for some clay from Mr. Chase. "Please, please give me some clay. I want to make something."

"What can you make? Are you a potter?" asked Mr. Chase.

"No, no. I want to make ducks, chickens, animals, people — statues."

Mr. Chase scratched his head. He had worked with clay all his life, making pots and vases but not ducks, chickens, or statues. Finally, he said, "All right. Get that bucket over there and fill it. That'll give you about twenty-five pounds of good clay."

Augusta took the clay home and immediately set to work making a statue. When Professor Mickens saw the statue, he said that she should teach a class in clay modeling. He got Mr. Chase to provide the clay for the class. And Professor Mickens also got the school board to agree to pay Augusta, still a student herself, a dollar a day for every day she taught.

In October 1921, Augusta started to take a four-year sculpture course at Cooper Union, a very fine art school in New York, where classes were free. Augusta passed the first year's course in one week and the second year's course in a month. But in February 1922, four months after she had begun, Augusta had to go to Miss Reynolds, the registrar. "I have to stop school," Augusta said sadly. "I have no more money. I have to get a job; otherwise I will be put out of my room."

Miss Reynolds told Augusta not to give up. Through a friend, Miss Reynolds immediately got Augusta a part-time job.

Then Miss Reynolds called a meeting of the advisory council of Cooper Union. Miss Reynolds asked the members if they were going to let a talented black woman, one of the first to study sculpture at Cooper Union, leave because she had no money. The council voted to pay for Augusta's room, board, and carfare. Augusta was never happier than when she learned that she could still attend classes.

Later in 1922, Augusta learned that the French government was going to open a summer art school outside Paris. Only one hundred American women students would be accepted. Augusta decided she wanted to go and paid thirty-five dollars to apply for the school. But her thirty-five dollars were returned. She was told that the selection committee was sorry that they could not accept her.

Augusta was badly hurt. She explained her story to some newspaper reporters. "I don't care much for myself," she said, "because I will get along all right here. But other and better black students may wish to apply sometime. The school is opening this year, and I am the first black woman to apply. I don't like to see the selection committee make a rule that may be used later."

Front-page stories about Augusta appeared day after day. Well-known people tried to get the committee to change its views. But it would not change them.

At this time, something else happened. Because of the newspaper stories, Augusta became the youngest nationally known sculptor. And she made many black people aware that they had fine artists and sculptors among themselves.

The problem of not having enough money still bothered Augusta. She was not able to support herself by selling her art pieces. So she worked in factories and in laundries. When she could, she kept working at her sculpture, making small figures and statues. Sometimes Augusta would sell some of them.

One day on a Harlem street, she met a young boy and asked him to pose for her. Quickly she modeled a head in clay, then scratched the title *Gamin* into its base. This is the French word meaning "a boy who lives in city streets."

Not long after *Gamin* was created, it was seen by Eugene Kinckle Jones of the National Urban League and

John E. Nail, well-known in Harlem real estate. They agreed that money had to be collected so that Augusta could have the chance to study under the best artists in Europe. Soon Augusta was in Paris studying the sculpture of faces and heads at one of the newest art schools.

On her return to the United States, Augusta again turned to making figures and statues of famous and ordinary people. She showed her pieces at many galleries, and she was the first black woman elected to the National Association of Women Painters and Sculptors.

Augusta Savage's last major work, "Lift Every Voice and Sing"

The Depression, which left twelve million Americans jobless, was to change the direction of her work. Not having enough money to create the kind of sculpture that she had once dreamed of, Augusta turned to spending most of her time teaching young black artists. Her home in Harlem became a center of creative activity. If a young boy or girl stopped by to see what was happening, Augusta cried, "Come on in." Opening her classes to anyone interested in painting, drawing, or carving, Augusta drew the gifted children of Harlem to her like a magnet. Soon she had sixty students working in her studio.

One of the talented youngsters she brought into her circle was Robert Jones, who had won a Fisher Bodies model contest. Augusta found ways to feed and house him and to include him in her classes. Norman Lewis was another student. Augusta taught him drawing and got him started in painting pictures. One day she was to see him become one of the leading modern painters in the United States.

The young artists worked hard to win her praise, her thoughtful and often sharp attention. She would stand for no foolishness. She told them that only through long, hard work would they become good artists.

When the Depression worsened and it became plain that jobs were needed, Augusta took a leading part in helping black artists to become enrolled in the Works Progress Administration art project. This United States government project provided jobs for painters and sculptors. By the mid-thirties, Augusta was in charge of one of the largest art centers in the government art programs, the Harlem Community Art Center.

Well-meaning friends pointed out that she was spending too much time working on government problems and teaching. But she told them, "I have made nothing really beautiful, really lasting. But if I can help these youngsters to develop the talent I know they have, then my monument will be in their work. No one could ask for more than that."

Augusta's last major work was for the 1939–1940 New York World's Fair. The song "Lift Every Voice" gave her the idea for her sculpture. She built a huge harp, sixteen feet tall. The strings of the harp came down from the heads of a line of singing black boys and girls. The base of the harp was formed by a large forearm and hand with the fingers curved gently upward. Augusta sculptured a kneeling black youth with outflung arms in front of the harp, offering the musical gifts of the black people to the world.

The World's Fair provided no money for casting the statue in bronze. Instead it was cast in plaster. Thousands of pictures of the statue were sent throughout the world, making it probably Augusta Savage's best known work, certainly the most widely seen. After the fair, because she had no money for casting the sculpture into bronze or for storing it, her work was smashed by bulldozers as part of the fair's cleanup.

Augusta Savage died on March 27, 1962. Five years later, three groups joined together to stage the largest show of the work of black artists ever held in the United States. Thousands of people came to see this exhibition. And the work that drew the most attention and the most favorable comments was *Gamin,* the head of a boy created by Augusta Savage.

Unfortunately, because Augusta could not afford to have her work cast in bronze, many of her statues have been damaged or destroyed. But the energy, under-standing, and insight she gave to her young black students live on. Their work *is* a monument to Augusta Savage.

I have always known
That at last I would
Take this road, but yesterday
I did not know that it would be today.

Narihira

All-Around Champion

The Life of Jim Thorpe

1888-1953

James Francis Thorpe and his twin brother, Charles, were born in 1888 on an Indian reservation. The area later became part of the state of Oklahoma. Jim's father was half Indian and half Irish. He could run, jump, and swim better than anyone else on the reservation. Jim's mother was the granddaughter of the famous Indian chief, Black Hawk. The Thorpes also had two older sons and two younger daughters.

Young Jim and Charlie loved the out-of-doors. The twins spent hours racing each other across their parents' 160-acre farmland. By the time the boys were four, they could ride and swim. But then, at the age of nine, Charlie died.

In 1904, when Jim was sixteen, he went to the Carlisle Indian School in Pennsylvania. It was an industrial school for Indians run by the federal government. Jim chose tailoring as the trade he wanted to learn.

One day Jim was watching the athletic coach, Glenn "Pop" Warner, work with the track team. Again and again, each boy tried to clear the high jump bar, set at five feet nine inches. Each boy made the short run, jumped into the air, kicked with his legs—and knocked the crossbar to the ground. "No, no!" the coach would yell. "You've got to *roll* over the bar."

Jim had never tried the high jump before, but he thought it looked easy. Finally the path to the bar was empty. Jim got up and started running. He jumped at just the right moment, clearing the bar with inches to spare. It was the first time anyone had done so all afternoon.

Pop Warner was impressed with Jim's jump that day. The following year, he put Jim on the varsity football team. During most of the season, however, Jim sat on the bench. But one day when the regular halfback was injured, Jim got his big chance. The small Carlisle school was playing the mighty University of Pennsylvania. In Jim's first try, he charged sixty-five yards for one touchdown and then eighty-five yards for a second! Before the football season was over, Jim Thorpe was the most talked-about player in Pennsylvania.

During the 1911 football season, Jim was the star of the team. In a game against unbeaten Harvard, he scored all of Carlisle's points, as they won 18-15. In Carlisle's game against Army, Jim ran ninety-seven yards for a touchdown and made twenty-two points. Carlisle beat Army, 27-6. Jim's record the next season was just as impressive, and, as a result, he was named to the All-American team both years. Pop Warner called his star athlete "the greatest football player of all time."

During the summer of 1909, Jim went with some of the other students to North Carolina. There they did some farm work and played baseball. Jim made fifteen dollars a week playing baseball—because he "liked to play ball." But years later, he would regret every penny he earned playing baseball that summer.

When Jim returned to Carlisle, Pop Warner told him that he had the potential for being an Olympic champion. Under Warner's coaching, Jim began to train.

The 1912 Olympics were held in Stockholm, Sweden. Jim entered the pentathlon and the decathlon. He won both!

The pentathlon is a five-event contest. It includes the running broad jump, javelin throw, 200-meter dash, discus throw, and the 1500-meter race. Jim came in first in four of the five events.

The decathlon is a ten-event contest. It covers all forms of track and field. The winner is considered the best all-around athlete in the world. Out of a possible 10,000 points, Jim scored 8,412. No one else came close to his amazing score!

For his accomplishments at the Olympics, Jim received many trophies and medals. Among them was a silver chalice presented to him by the King of Sweden.

Back in the United States, Jim was a hero. He was honored all over the country for his performance at the Olympics.

203

When Jim finished school at Carlisle in 1913, he became a baseball player for the New York Giants. But then his troubles began. Jim received a letter asking him to appear before the American Athletic Union to answer charges brought against him.

During the course of the inquiry, it was brought out that Jim had accepted money for playing ball. That made him a professional athlete, and professionals were not allowed to compete in the Olympics. As a result, Jim had to return all his Olympic awards, and his name was removed from all the records. It was as though he had never even been to the Olympics.

Pop Warner and Jim tried to appeal the decision of the A.A.U. But they were turned down.

Jim played professional baseball until 1919. In 1920, he helped start what later became the National Football League. In 1925, at the age of thirty-seven, he was the star of the New York Giants football team.

Jim retired from professional sports in 1929. The next several years were hard ones. He tried many things—lecturing on sports and on Indian culture; helping the Sac and Fox Indians back in Oklahoma; and doing bit parts in Hollywood westerns. In 1932, he was working as a laborer in Los Angeles, California.

The 1932 Olympics were to be held in Los Angeles. But Jim could not even afford a ticket. Somehow, people found out about Jim. Hundreds offered him their tickets. The Vice-President of the United States, Charles Curtis, himself part Indian, also heard about Jim's plight. He invited Jim to join him in the presidential box. At the opening ceremony, one hundred thousand fans gave Jim Thorpe a standing ovation. He had not been forgotten.

Jim Thorpe was remembered again in 1950. The 393 sportswriters and broadcasters of the Associated Press were asked their opinions on two questions: Who did they think was the greatest football player, and who did they think was the greatest male athlete of the first half of the 1900's? When the results of the polls were announced, Jim had won them both. No one could ever beat the mighty Jim Thorpe!

Good Boy, Knute

by Max Kase

There are few people who will argue the fact that the late Knute Rockne, of Notre Dame fame, was the sharpest wit football ever produced. Some of his stories are well-known and will remain so for years to come.

From his experience both as a player and a coach, he told interesting stories of the football field, and there were many times when "the Rock" himself was the butt of a joke.

There was the time when he was assigned to stop the greatest football player of them all — the mighty Jim Thorpe, of the Carlisle Indians. Rockne was an end on the Notre Dame football team. When this team played the terrific Carlisle team, coached by "Pop" Warner, it was Rockne's job to tackle Thorpe. Three times he succeeded in stopping the big Indian. After the third time, Thorpe smiled pleasantly and said, "Be a good boy. Let Jim run."

Thorpe took the ball again, and Rockne went after him.

"Never before have I received such a shock," Rockne said. "It was as if a locomotive had hit me, followed by a ten-ton truck rambling over the remains. I lay on the field of battle while Thorpe rounded out a forty-yard run for a touchdown.

"After the run, Thorpe came back, helped me to my feet, patted me on the back, and, grinning broadly, said, 'That's a good boy, Knute. You let Jim run.'"

SWIM FOR LIFE

by William M. Stephens

Joe and his daughter, Rita, had been below the surface of the water for half an hour when the storm hit. In the middle of the afternoon, Joe had anchored the boat over Turtle Reef. Then he and Rita had put on scuba gear to hunt for the big fish that lay under the ledges forty feet down. Rita had just learned how to breathe underwater with an air tank strapped to her back. So she stayed at about twenty feet while her father worked the bottom of the reef, looking under the rocks for fish.

Joe was beneath a ledge with only his legs sticking out when he felt a tug on one flipper. Surprised, he backed out quickly. Instead of being happy to see Rita and not a shark, he was angry and worried. She shouldn't have come down so deep. Joe jerked his thumb roughly toward the surface, then indicated with his hand that Rita shouldn't rise too fast. Rita, however, had already started up and was waving her arms excitedly, pointing toward the surface. Joe realized that the water had turned dark. The rays from the sun no longer bounced off the white, sandy bottom.

Joe rose to the surface, and a breaking wave slapped his face. Large drops of rain were falling, and a strong wind was blowing from the land.

"Where is the boat?" Joe shouted. "You should have watched the boat! We've drifted away from it." Rita,

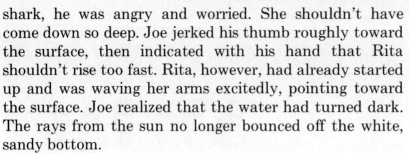

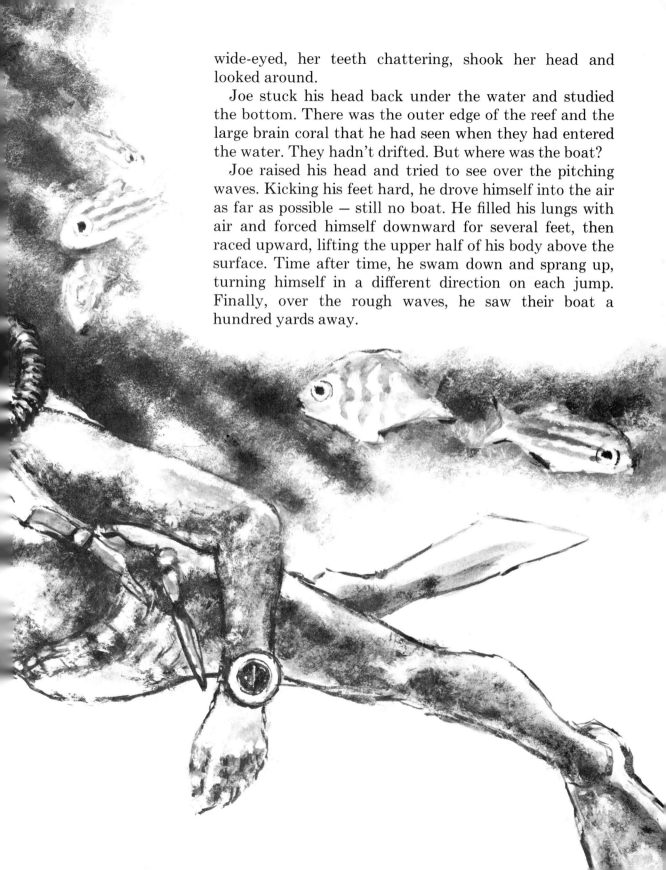

wide-eyed, her teeth chattering, shook her head and looked around.

Joe stuck his head back under the water and studied the bottom. There was the outer edge of the reef and the large brain coral that he had seen when they had entered the water. They hadn't drifted. But where was the boat?

Joe raised his head and tried to see over the pitching waves. Kicking his feet hard, he drove himself into the air as far as possible — still no boat. He filled his lungs with air and forced himself downward for several feet, then raced upward, lifting the upper half of his body above the surface. Time after time, he swam down and sprang up, turning himself in a different direction on each jump. Finally, over the rough waves, he saw their boat a hundred yards away.

"It's over there!" he shouted. Then came a chilling real-ization: The stern of the boat was toward the wind. They had anchored it at the bow!

"The boat is adrift, Rita!" he shouted. "It has broken loose. Wait here." Pulling the release strap on his weight belt, Joe dropped it as he started to swim. Slowed by the heavy air tank on his back, Joe paused after a few strokes to remove it. "Take care of this!" he called, pushing the tank in Rita's direction. Then, disappointed, he watched it sink from sight. How could he be so stupid? He should have known that the tank still held too much air for it to float.

There wasn't time to dive for the tank. He had to get to the boat. So he pulled his snorkel tube from his belt and jammed the mouthpiece between his teeth. Then he struck out again, kicking hard with his legs. He felt him-self rise and fall as he plowed through the high swells.

Joe swam hard for a full minute, then kicked himself upward to check on his progress. The boat was as far away as ever. He looked for Rita but couldn't see her over the dancing waves. In the driving rain, he couldn't even see Key Alto, which lay five miles behind him. For a moment, he became really frightened.

"Take it easy, Joe," he told himself. "You can catch that boat. Turn loose the spear gun and make some time. You've lost twenty feet by stopping to look. Swim, man, swim!"

He dropped the spear gun, freeing both arms for swim-ming. He watched the gun as it sank. A cloud of sand rose when it hit the bottom. "The water is thirty feet deep," he thought. "Soon it gets deeper."

Then he noticed small puffs of sand, like brown smoke, on the bottom. The puffs were in a line in the sand. Those marks were made by the dragging anchor! He wouldn't have to waste time now by stopping to check his bearings. The boat was straight ahead, but how far?

He raced hard for five minutes — ten minutes — follow-ing the trail of the dragging anchor. Without slowing his pace, Joe could read the dial on his waterproof watch. His arms and legs ached.

"I'm heading straight out to sea," he thought. "The bottom is shelving off. How far is the drop-off of the ocean floor and the beginning of really deep water?"

He tried to guess how far he had swum. "I can swim maybe two miles an hour, and the current is moving at least three miles an hour. The strong current is helping me swim faster. The drop-off is seven or eight miles from the reef . . . or about twelve miles from shore. How far have I come?"

Then Joe thought about Rita. He hoped she would let the air out of the tank so she could have something to hold on to and not drown.

Thirty minutes passed. Suddenly he felt an almost overpowering desire to turn around and head for shore. He began to argue with himself. Part of his mind seemed to shout, *"Go back. Go back while there's still time."*

"But we'll both drown if I turn around," answered Joe.

"You can still make it to shore," his mind reminded him.

"Never. The current is too strong," argued Joe.

"The current will slow down. You can rest until it does. You can float without using a single muscle. Float and rest. Then swim to shore. You're not gaining on the boat, Joe."

"What about Rita? Without the boat I'll never find her," Joe told himself.

"Rita is gone, Joe. Accept it. You'll never find her. This is a big ocean."

"Shut up!" Joe told his mind. "I'm gaining on the boat. I know I am. I'll find Rita. I just hope she can let the air out of the tank. I can't remember whether I ever showed her how."

Fifteen minutes sped by. Joe hadn't slowed his stroke for an instant. His shoulders no longer hurt. His arms seemed like the whirling blades of a windmill, driven by some outside force.

Suddenly he felt he couldn't stand much more. The strong power of his arms and the kick of his feet hadn't slowed, but the puffs of sand below seemed no larger. He fought against a sense of despair. How easy it would be to relax — to stop swimming. *"Relax and think of nothing. Relax and sleep,"* his mind said.

"No! No! Rita is back there. She trusts me. She's waiting," Joe screamed.

The water was now about fifty feet deep. He wasn't far from the drop-off. Soon he'd see scattered patches of coral. Perhaps the anchor would hang up in one of them. . . .

The water seemed calmer. Had the wind stopped blowing?

"How can a boat be so important? It's only made from plywood. I'd gladly cast the boat adrift if I could use it only long enough to find Rita," Joe said to himself.

He swam through a school of large jellyfish. They swept on him in a rush. He felt the jellyfish sting his skin as they brushed against his body. One struck him full on the mouth and moved slowly down his neck and chest. Tomorrow there would be great big red bumps on his face and body.

Joe's mind began to play tricks. Objects seemed to brush against his legs, and he felt that a school of great sharks was following him. "Oh, no," he thought. "I won't look around. I don't have time."

He felt that he was fighting his way through a maze of cobwebs. "But there aren't any cobwebs in the sea," he told himself.

"How do you know? You've never swum out this far before," said a part of his mind.

Large bunches of seaweed floated past him. Ahead he saw what appeared to be a large clump of seaweed resting on the bottom. He could not make out the shape, but it reminded him of a bale of hay. He watched the clump for several minutes. He seemed to get no nearer to it. At times, the mass appeared to roll over.

He wondered if a mass of seaweed could be dragged across the bottom of the ocean by a current. If so, there's more current on the bottom than he'd ever seen — more than on top. He was swimming hard, but he wasn't gaining.

He had been swimming for more than an hour now. The drop-off couldn't be far ahead. He had to increase his speed. The thought sent pain spreading through his body. *"You're doing all right. Why speed up now? Your motor is running smoothly,"* his mind told him.

"I've got to catch that bale of hay. Move, arms, move. Kick, legs, kick. Shoot the works, body," Joe told himself.

"Who's kidding whom?" his mind questioned. *"You've shot the works."*

"I'll shoot them again. Increase the speed," Joe shouted.

"You haven't got it," his mind said.

"Pour on the fuel then."

"The fuel is gone," Joe's mind told him.

"Come on; increase the speed," Joe shouted again.

By a painful force of will, Joe speeded up. He could feel his muscles tighten and protest at his change in pace. His stomach was knotted. His mind said, *"Your body can't take it, Skipper. It will shake itself to pieces."*

"Go ahead. I'll get new parts at the next port," Joe said.

"Bimini? You're a card, Joe."

Joe knew he was going faster. The object was larger and clearer. Finally, he could see a line curving upward. The bale of hay was his anchor! Dragging across the bottom of the ocean, the anchor had picked up a mass of seaweed.

Inch by inch, Joe gained. He still couldn't see the boat. The anchor line was one hundred feet long. Joe was about thirty or forty feet away from it. If he could get hold of that line, . . .

Soon he was directly over the anchor. Then he passed it. The line stretched below him, only twenty feet away. He thought to himself, "Now is the time to get the line. I'm nearly at the drop-off. If I don't get the anchor, it will drop straight down. I've just got to get that line now. If I only had a long boathook, . . . "

His mind told him, *"Why don't you dive for the line, Joe? You're a diver. Just dive straight down."*

"What if I miss the line?" Joe wondered.

"Why would you miss it?"

"Because I haven't much air," Joe said to himself.

"You don't need air. That rope is only twenty feet away."

"I've been swimming so long," Joe muttered.

"Are you bragging?" his mind asked. *"Get the line."*

Joe filled his burning lungs, upended, and kicked downward. His chest ached, and his head pounded. Finally he touched the rope, but it slipped away. He needed air badly. But he wouldn't have a second chance to get that rope. He kicked his feet hard and grabbed the line with both hands. It ran through his fingers. Then suddenly, the anchor hit his hands, and he held it tightly.

Then he finned upward, holding the anchor with both hands. Up, up, up . . . He wondered, "How can a ten-pound anchor weigh a hundred pounds?"

Joe reached the surface, gasping for air.

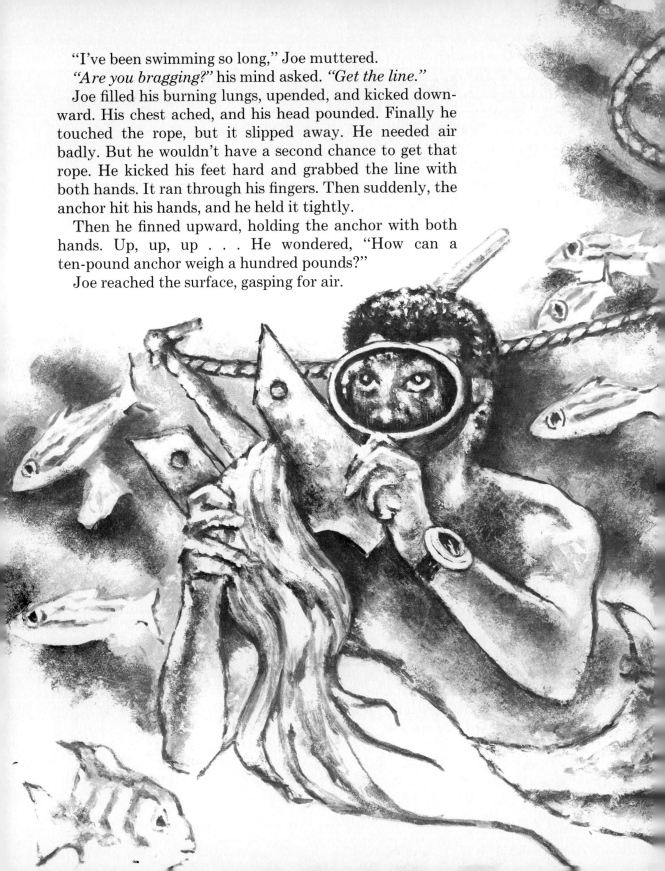

The weight of the anchor pulled him down while the moving boat dragged him forward. He kicked his legs desperately, trying to hold his head up. He tried to untie the knot that held the anchor to the rope, but the knot was too tight. His fingers wouldn't bend, but he knew they'd hold on to the rope.

After a minute of kicking to support the heavy weight of the anchor, Joe took a deep breath and let himself be carried under. He relaxed all but his arm muscles for four, five, six seconds. Then he pulled himself forward, gaining several feet of line before surfacing for some more air. Inch by inch, he worked himself up the line, letting the anchor slip through his hands toward the bottom. Then he felt the downward pulling stop as the anchor hit the bottom of the ocean.

Joe was within thirty feet of the boat. He took the rope and made a half-hitch knot around his arm to let himself be dragged to his goal. With his weight on the line, the boat slowly swung around until the bow was facing him. He was glad to see the boarding ladder still hung over the side. Without the ladder, he'd never make it.

Joe felt a great need for rest, but the thought of Rita gave him the will to go on. "I've got to get into the boat. Then I can rest as I drive it back."

His arms and legs didn't want to move. Every muscle ached. He doubled up his body, then straightened it, keeping his feet together. Three kicks, four kicks, and he was at the boat. Inch by inch, he climbed up the ladder and into the boat.

He sank on one knee, breathing in long, gasping sobs. *"Get the motor started, then rest,"* his mind ordered him.

Joe turned on the gas and pulled the choke. He yanked at the starter cord, but it slipped from his grasp. He braced one foot and pulled with both hands. "I can't pull it. I'm as weak as a kitten," he said. Then Joe sank to the floorboards and lay without moving. He seemed to be still beating the water with his arms.

Finally his chest stopped pounding, and the triphammer beat of his heart slowed. He took off his flippers and mask, wrapped a towel around his hands, braced both feet, and pulled with all his weight on the cord. The motor caught.

Joe turned the bow westward. He had no compass and couldn't see land. The sun, low in the afternoon sky, was a good guide, however. Land was toward the sun.

Then he remembered the anchor. Slowing the motor, Joe went forward and pulled at the line. He had strength only to raise the anchor to the water line. Strain as he might, he couldn't lift it into the boat. He wound the line around a cleat and let the anchor hang over the side. At least it wouldn't drag on the bottom.

Several inches of water washed around Joe's feet. He used a bucket to scoop up the water and toss it over the side. The boat was soon dry, and it skimmed smoothly over the long swells. Shortly, Joe saw land — Conch Point and, farther south, a span of the Overseas Highway.

He began to look for Rita about two miles before reaching Turtle Reef. He was sure his daughter couldn't have held her position against the wind and tide.

A plane flew over, high. He wished that he had a radio. Planes or helicopters could spot a small girl at sea in the remaining two hours of daylight. He felt blind. "I'll never find her," he thought.

His eyes searched the sea. He stood on the seat, his head as high as possible. The water was now smooth, but the glare of the low sun made spotting a small object almost impossible. Rita might be anywhere in an area of ten square miles —maybe more.

Joe looked toward the shore and made a decision. There were radios and telephones at Alto Fish Camp, where he and Rita had set out from. With about two hours of daylight left, his best chance was to go there and call the Coast Guard.

Joe sped toward shore. Now, inside the reef, the water was less than twenty feet deep.

He saw a small object out of the corner of one eye. It was several hundred feet away. It was like a floating log, with a smaller object alongside — a log and a coconut.

With his hair rising on the back of his neck — afraid to hope, afraid to know — Joe moved closer. "My eyes are playing tricks. No, it's a tank, all right . . . and a head. She can't be alive, but let her be!" he thought.

It *was* the back of Rita's head. An arm was flung across the diving tank. Then Joe noticed that something was odd. Rita's head didn't float with the current. The tide made a V-shaped wake as it moved past the tank and the girl's head.

Joe was twenty feet away from her. Rita moved, turned in his direction, raised a small hand, and waved.

The strain within Joe released like a broken spring. He wanted to cry. His shoulders shook as he eased the boat alongside.

Rita grabbed the ladder. "Here," Rita gasped. "Take the tank and the spear gun." She climbed aboard, pulled off her mask, and grinned weakly. Her lips and chin were blue, and a red circle marked the spot where her diving mask had pushed against her face. "Oh, am I glad to see you, Dad!" she said, shivering. "I thought you'd never get back!"

Joe tried to find words. Instead, he gripped his daughter's shoulders. "Rita," he finally croaked, "how did you ever get inside the reef? How did you fight the current?"

"Well," Rita said slowly, "I tried to figure out what you'd do. I had to stay near the reef, or you'd never find me. So I let the air out of the tank and used it as a float, pushing it ahead of me. After I got tired of swimming against the current, I tried shooting the spear into the bottom and using it as an anchor. Since the line from the spear was fastened to the gun, all I had to do was hold onto the gun to keep from drifting away. It was easy after I reached shallow water. The spear really holds between those rocks."

Joe turned away so that Rita couldn't see his face. "I will never forget . . . I will never forget this afternoon," he thought.

ADMIRAL: **Why is the sea measured in knots?**
SAILOR: **To keep the ocean tide.**

219

BERMUDA TRIANGLE

by Charles F. Berlitz

Much has been written about the strange happenings in the area known as the Bermuda Triangle. This is one man's account.

There is a place in the Atlantic Ocean, near the southern coast of Florida, where ships and airplanes seem to disappear more often than any other place on Earth. This area is called the Bermuda Triangle. The Triangle is formed by Miami, Bermuda, and the ocean east of Puerto Rico. Since 1945, over one hundred planes and ships and over one thousand persons have disappeared from there. It is almost as if the lost planes had flown into a hole in the sky or the ships had been suddenly drawn down into a huge whirlpool or been taken from the surface of the sea. The strangest thing about these disappearances is that nothing has been found — no survivors, no life belts or lifeboats or life rafts, no wreckage, and no oil slick on the water.

BERMUDA

BERMUDA TRIANGLE

PUERTO RICO

The biggest single loss of planes happened in December 1945. Five Navy planes from Fort Lauderdale, Florida, were flying together with a total crew of fourteen. The pilots radioed back to their base that their flying instruments were not working and that they did not know where they were. The base radioed back to them to follow the sun west. But they replied that they could not see the sun, although the weather was good, and that even the ocean "didn't look as it should." Finally, they said they could not hear the base. But the base tower could still hear them talking about strange "white water." The last thing the tower heard was, "Don't come after us. . . . It looks like . . . " Then there was silence. In the meantime, a rescue plane with a crew of thirteen was sent to help them. But the crew on the rescue plane sent one message: It was approaching the place where the planes were lost. Then, when it entered the area, it also disappeared and was never heard from again. After an investigation lasting many months, a Navy officer said, "It's a complete mystery. It's almost as if the planes had flown to Mars."

Sometimes a plane or a ship has disappeared right after sending a message saying that everything was okay. During the 1963 Christmas season, the pilot of a DC-3 passenger plane bound for Miami asked the control tower for landing instructions. Then the pilot said to the tower, "Would you believe it? The passengers are still singing Christmas carols!" Then suddenly the plane's radio went off the air. Neither the plane, its crew, nor its passengers were ever heard from again.

It is known that pilots of planes often have trouble with their instruments within the Bermuda Triangle. Sometimes the compasses and radar don't work or the radio goes out. This may explain why some planes get lost and crash. But it does not explain why some planes vanish in good weather or when they are coming in for a landing.

Many people have studied the area of the Bermuda Triangle to find out what could cause the strange happenings there. In 1965, a Navy plane was sent to investigate the magnetic field within the area. But shortly after the plane flew into the Triangle, it disappeared with its crew of ten.

Most of the ships and planes have vanished close to land in good weather and often in the daylight. Whatever happens seems to happen very quickly. A small yacht named *Witchcraft* disappeared right off Miami Harbor. Its owner, Dan Burack, had anchored at Buoy No. 9 to admire the Christmas lights in Miami. Suddenly, he sent a call for help to the Coast Guard but did not say what was wrong. As a Coast Guard cutter sped to Buoy No. 9, the Coast Guard crew heard Burack say on the radio, "I've never seen one like that before." Nobody knows what he meant. By the time the Coast Guard cutter arrived at Buoy No. 9, the *Witchcraft* and its passengers had disappeared.

Many large ships have vanished as well, one weighing twenty thousand tons and another with more than three hundred people on board. The crew on one Japanese freighter sent a very strange last message, saying, "Danger like dagger now. Come quickly! We cannot escape." After this message, there were no more. The ship has never been found.

Some of the ships that have disappeared could have been turned over by a sudden tidal wave or been blown up by an explosion. Or a small boat could have been run into and sunk by a larger one, although this does not seem possible. In any case, something would have been left in the sea, either wreckage or an oil slick.

It is strange that many small and large ships have been found adrift without their crew and passengers or any clue to where the people could have gone. These empty drifting ships are still another mystery. The ships' cargoes are often still in place, and the lifeboats are still on board. But as for the people, it is almost as if they were suddenly taken away into the sea or into the sky. Sometimes a single animal is left on board — on one ship, a dog; on another, a cat; and on still another, a canary in a cage. Only once did a nonhuman disappear along with the people. That was a parrot.

Some pilots and ship captains in the Bermuda Triangle

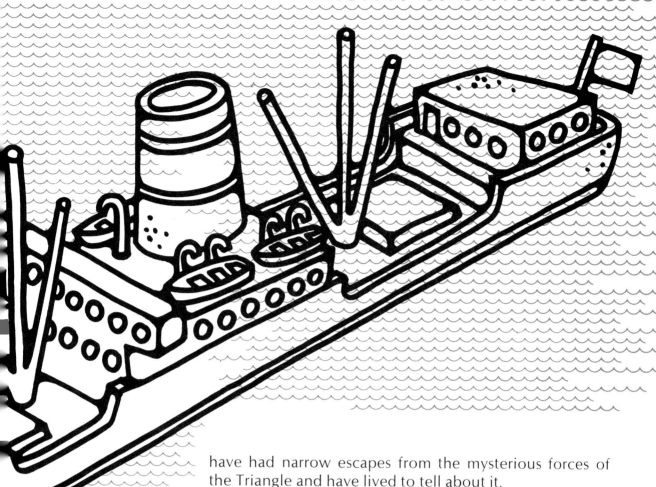

have had narrow escapes from the mysterious forces of the Triangle and have lived to tell about it.

A pilot named Chuck Wakeley was returning to Florida from the Bahama Islands in the early evening when he noticed that his instruments were "going crazy" and that he could not control his plane. Then he saw that the wings were glowing a greenish-white color and that the instrument panel glowed so brightly that he could not look at it. Finally, he seemed to be glowing himself. Then the greenish-white glow stopped, and he could control his plane again. When Wakeley talked to other pilots about his strange experience, he realized that he had flown into the midst of the mysterious forces of the Bermuda Triangle.

Captain Don Henry was towing another boat over a deep part of the Atlantic Ocean near the Bahamas. The weather was clear, but suddenly a mist appeared around

the boat he was pulling, and he started to be pulled backward, having a sort of tug-of-war with an unknown force.
Captain Henry lost all his electric power, but using diesel
power, he pulled the boat free from the mist. Later, he
found that fifty flashlight batteries were useless because
all the electricity had been drained from them.

Another ship, *Wild Goose,* also in tow, was not so
lucky. It suddenly was covered by a mist and pulled underwater with five people on board. Only one person escaped. He was resting in a cabin when he suddenly found
himself underwater. He escaped through a porthole and
swam to the surface, where the towboat rescued him. The
towboat crew told him that his ship had vanished in the
glowing mist as if it had been sucked under by a whirlpool. The towboat crew had cut their lines so they would
not be pulled under too.

But where have all the planes, ships, and people gone?
The United States Navy, the Coast Guard, and many insurance companies have looked into this matter for many
years. But they have found no answers. It cannot even be
said that the people who were on board the vanishing

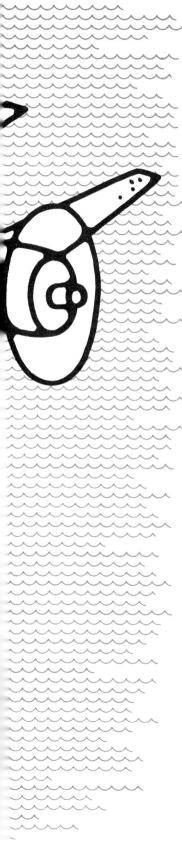

planes and ships have died. The body of anyone who has disappeared has never been found.

Some people who have studied the mystery think that parts of the Bermuda Triangle may be a magnetic-force field or a pathway to another place, that is, a road out of our world leading into another world. They point out that more UFO's (Unidentified Flying Objects) — often called "flying saucers" — have been seen along the southern coast of Florida and the Bahamas than in any other part of the world. They suggest that perhaps the UFO's come into our world along this pathway and capture the planes and ships.

Others think that the UFO's may come from underwater, and they point out that many mysterious things have been seen underwater by pilots and ship captains in the clear waters of the Bermuda Triangle. For example, an underwater object, like a small submarine, was reported as heading directly for a ship at a rate much faster than the submarines we know — but at the last minute the object turned aside. In 1963, an underwater object was tracked by a fleet of ships for several days at speeds up to one hundred fifty knots an hour and at depths up to twenty-seven thousand feet, which is about five miles. But there are no submarines that we know of that can go as fast and as deep.

Many ships and planes cross the Bermuda Triangle every day. Yet nothing happens to them. Since so many planes, ships, and people have vanished without a reason, this area is thought of as one of the most mysterious in the world. Perhaps some day, when more is known about the forces in the world, the mystery of the Bermuda Triangle will be solved.

Survival Skills
Reading a Graph and a Chart

A Line Graph

If you do not already drive a car, you probably will learn to drive soon. However, before you can get your driver's license, you must pass a test. To pass the test, you must show that you can drive a car. Also, you must show that you know the state's laws of the road. Perhaps you will take a driver-education course that will teach you how to drive. If you do, one of the things you will learn about is highway safety. Graphs and charts may be used in your course to show you facts about driving.

In a very small space, a graph can sometimes give more facts than words can. On a graph, you can see information at a glance. You can easily compare the facts given in a graph.

Look at the line graph on the next page. This graph was made by the police department of Berryville. The title tells the kind of information this graph shows: the number of highway accidents that occurred at different speeds in May. On the left side of the graph are the numbers 10, 20, 30, and 40. These count the number of accidents by 10's. At the bottom of the graph is a row of numbers counted by 10's up to Over 60. These numbers show the speed at which the accidents happened. Now notice the colored line that goes from left to right on the graph. This line shows the relationship between the Number of Accidents and the Speed in Miles Per Hour. Any point on the colored line stands for a fact. Look at the point that has been marked with an X. Put your right index finger on the X. The X is in the 30 column of Speed in Miles Per Hour. Now move your finger to the left to the Number of Accidents. What is the number your finger is

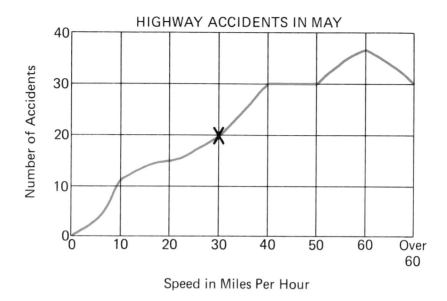

HIGHWAY ACCIDENTS IN MAY

Number of Accidents (vertical axis: 0, 10, 20, 30, 40)

Speed in Miles Per Hour (horizontal axis: 0, 10, 20, 30, 40, 50, 60, Over 60)

on now? Yes, the number of accidents is 20. Now, put these facts together. What do they tell you? There were 20 traffic accidents that happened while the driver was going 30 miles per hour.

Now look at the graph again. How many accidents took place while the driver was going 20 miles per hour? Put your right index finger on the colored line where it crosses the 20 column of Speed in Miles Per Hour. Now move your finger to the left to the Number of Accidents. Your finger should be in the middle of the space between 10 and 20. You know that the number of accidents is counted by 10's. What number is halfway between 10 and 20? That's right, 15. So, 15 accidents happened while the driver was going 20 miles per hour.

A Chart

A chart is sometimes called a table. Like a graph, a chart is used to show facts at a glance. A chart gives information that you can compare. A chart can show something in less space than it would take to use a lot of words to explain the same thing.

CAUSES OF HIGHWAY ACCIDENTS, APRIL–JUNE

Cause	April	May	June
Driving too fast	27	30	22
Carelessness	6	5	4
Drunken driving	10	15	21
Engine failure	8	1	3
Poor weather conditions	12	9	4
Total	63	60	54

Look at the chart above. The police department of Berryville made this chart to show the causes of highway accidents that happened in April, May, and June. Where do you get that information? That's right, from the title. Read the heading of each column at the top of the chart. Now read the first cause of highway accidents during this three-month period. How many accidents happened in each month because of driving too fast? In April, 27 accidents happened; in May, 30 accidents happened; and in June, 22 accidents happened by driving too fast.

Now let's look at the number of accidents caused by engine failure. You can see that 8 accidents occurred in April, 1 in May, and 3 in June. This chart shows that there were more than twice as many accidents caused by engine failure in April as there were in June.

Let's say that in May, all automobiles had to be inspected by a garage. Does that give you a clue to the story behind the facts? What might it mean? Yes, it might mean that people had their car engines fixed in May so that their cars would pass inspection. Sometimes you can apply a fact that you know to help you understand the facts given in a chart.

Look at the bottom of the chart. The last line gives the total number of accidents that happened in each of the three months. Which month had the most accidents? That's right, April.

Now use the line graph and the chart to answer each of the following questions. Use a separate piece of paper. Write the number of each question and the letter of the correct answer.

1. According to the graph, at which speed do most accidents happen?
    a. 50 miles per hour   c. over 60 miles per hour
    b. 40 miles per hour   d. 60 miles per hour

2. According to the graph, about how many accidents took place at 35 miles per hour?
    a. 25   c. 20
    b. 30   d. 40

3. Look at the chart. Which cause resulted in the fewest number of accidents for the three-month period?
    a. carelessness   c. poor weather conditions
    b. engine failure   d. drunken driving

4. According to the chart, what was the *second* greatest cause of accidents in April?
    a. drunken driving   c. carelessness
    b. driving too fast   d. poor weather conditions

5. According to the chart, in which month were there the fewest accidents?
    a. April
    b. May
    c. June

DIARY OF THE HAUTER EXPERIMENT

by Bernice Grohskopf

Evelyn B. Chestnut keeps a diary of her life in a timeless world of perfect order, in which she is trapped. Although at first she found the gleaming, noiseless, and orderly new world interesting, she now wants to escape. But can she?

24th Day

Today there was a dancing class for the first time. The TV teacher directed us to move chairs and desks to the side of the room. Then we started warm-ups, like bending, stretching, sitting on the floor, and touching our foreheads to our knees. We did the sort of thing my mom is always trying to do and telling me I should start doing now, while I'm young. Anyway, the teacher's voice told us exactly what to do, and instead of a real person on the screen, there was a drawing of a figure showing the movements. We were all groaning, except for my friend Drucy. She could do all the things easily. She just moved as though she were a flower in the wind. She's tall with a long neck and a long thin body. She seemed to know that we were all watching her, so her movements got better. By just watching her and not the TV figure, we all found it easier. She had such a nice look on her face, very smooth and grown-up and — I don't know how to describe it, but her eyes were quiet. Her face looked like someone who had just discovered something beautiful, or like a person remembering joy, all quiet and happy.

The class seemed to last for the usual amount of time, and we were all facing Drucy by the time the class ended and the red light started to blink. Drucy saw the light and looked at us sitting on the floor. We were all out of breath. The look on her face suddenly changed, and her eyes got deep and serious. You could tell she was going to say something important. So we sat very still, waiting, and Drucy leaned forward and said in a loud whisper, "Listen, kids, if we stick together, we can get out of here."

No one said a word. We just looked at one another, hardly moving our heads. Then Drucy said, still talking in a loud whisper, "I have an idea. After dinner tonight, we . . ." She stopped. I remember the room was still as the kids leaned forward to hear her. That's when it happened! I can hardly describe it now without getting all sick and sweaty from the memory. The TV wall started to flash a million bright blinking lights and colors, like a bad dream that makes you feel dizzy. I remember a terrible noise, the shrill noise of metal scraping on metal, like the shrieking of the subway. And the smell! Oh, it was awful. I don't even want to remember it.

I don't know how long it lasted. And nobody will talk about it now. I think it happened today, but we got so confused. Nobody knew how long we'd been sitting there with the noise and smell and flashing lights. At some point, everything got quiet, and the smell went away, and the lights stopped, and we just all got up to go to the next class. But everyone was very shaky, and we'd all been very quiet. Hardly anyone was talking,

even in the social room and the cafeteria, where mostly everyone talked a little. The place was like a funeral parlor. Everyone was acting very obediently. We knew we were being watched every second.

Drucy and I had noticed that one of the tile squares on the floor of the cafeteria looked a little different from the others. One tile was loose. Tonight, when everyone was asleep, we planned to try to lift the square and escape.

I waited in bed, in the darkness, for Drucy to come and give me the signal. At first, it seemed to me the room would never quiet down. The kids were restless, turning over, and sighing and groaning. I was afraid Drucy would be so impatient that she'd get up too soon and blow the whole thing. But she didn't, of course. After a while, everything was quiet, just sounds of steady breathing and strange little wheezings. That went on for so long that I began to wonder if Drucy had fallen asleep. I couldn't keep my mind on a single thing. All I could think of was what I'd do if, after we were able to lift out that big square in the cafeteria, we saw someone looking up at us. All sorts of terrible, mad-looking faces began to form in my mind. I had flashes of remembering all the goofy fright movies I'd seen on TV. I was getting myself so scared that I decided I'd better try to think of something else. So, I tried to count. That got so dull. Then I tried to remember the names of all the states in the United States. Finally, I heard a faint rustling, and I knew it had to be Drucy getting out of bed.

I sat up on my bed and waited. I had the ruler in my hand. Then she reached out and touched me. I could barely make out her face. I started to follow her, holding onto her finger tips lightly. She signaled me, with pressure on my shoulder, to bend down, though I didn't know why. As we reached the door, our grip on each other's fingers tightened, and we both held our breath. We slipped through without making a sound and, still crouching, crept along the hall to the cafeteria. It seemed like a mile. We were as quiet as mice.

The cafeteria was dim but not dark. We hurried over to the place where the loose tile was and kneeled down, almost as though we were going to say our prayers. For a few minutes, I guess we did. Then, I tried to slip the ruler in the crack to lift the block up, but it didn't work. Drucy got impatient and grabbed it from me. I groped around the floor until I found the knife that Drucy had brought along, and then every time she'd get the square lifted up just a little, I'd grab it with my fingers and try to hold it and stick the knife in under it. But the square kept slipping

down again. We kept working, but we were too nervous and excited and frightened to do anything right. We were beginning to get on each other's nerves, blaming each other without saying a word, just giving looks of fury. But, at last, we got a good hold and lifted the whole square out. It was much lighter than I'd expected, as though it were made of cork. We put it down silently. My heart was going so fast and loud I thought I was going to split. I was so scared, expecting something awful to reach up and grab us.

The big surprise was that when we looked down the opening, it wasn't dark. It was very bright — all shiny and clean, just like everything else in the place, with a bright green carpeted staircase leading down. For a few minutes, we just looked down, kneeling at the opening, wondering which one should go down first. I was wondering if we should both go down and try to pull the block back in place. Then Drucy whispered that we should both go down and not bother about the block — to just leave the opening.

Drucy went first, creeping carefully down the carpeted stairway, me behind her, my heart pounding

like a thousand horses' hoofs. At the bottom of the staircase, we both looked back up at the same time. It looked so strange — that opening into the darkness.

At the bottom of the steps was a narrow white hallway and a white door without any handle. We both looked at it; then I saw Drucy take a deep breath, press her lips together, and close her eyes as she pushed very gently. There was no sound. Carefully, we poked our heads in first and looked into a huge, gleaming kitchen. It was like one of those shining laboratories in a science-fiction movie, with everything bright chrome and stainless steel and white tile or glass. The ceiling was all glass panels with lights behind them, so it was like sunshine when we stepped in.

We moved slowly into the room and stood for a while looking around. I don't know how long we stood there taking in all the glass-enclosed shelves with dishes and glasses and stacks of plastic trays. I noticed the moving belt that brought our trays up to the cafeteria. After a while, Drucy started to move toward another door at the end of the kitchen. As I tiptoed behind Drucy, I kept thinking of how we always had used the word "they" when we talked about the mysterious people who were behind all that was happening upstairs. Now I was wondering when we were going to meet "they." Which door were they behind?

As Drucy pushed the door open, we again leaned our heads in to look first before we moved. This room looked like a sort of fancy meeting room, not as big as the kitchen. It looked like the kind of room shown in the movies when there's an important business meeting. This room also had a ceiling with all glass and lights, and there was a big, round shining table with seven blue leather chairs around it. Drucy and I looked at one another, then looked back at the empty chairs, wondering who sat in them, and when. On one wall, there were bookshelves filled with books that had all the same bindings, sort of blue leather with gold letters. Then we noticed a book on the table in front of the chair at the far end of the table.

Drucy touched the book, then turned the cover to the first page. All it said was *The Hauter Experiment* by Franz Bruno Hauter. She turned the page, and we started to read it.

A timeless world of perfect order, free of all fear or worry. There will be no pressure of time. The students will live in a perfectly ordered, controlled routine world. Life will alternate between hours of study and learning, recreation, rest, physical exercise, and sleep. All needs, such as laundry and cooking, will be taken care of for them in ways that will cause them the least possible concern. An air-cleaning system, always in use, will keep the air germ-free, so there will be no disease.

"Changing Behavior"
Measures to Follow
(See Chapter VI for measures to be taken in emergency.)

At that point, Drucy looked at me, her eyes wide. I realized I'd been holding my breath almost all the while we'd been reading. For a few minutes, we listened for sounds, then we read on.

Each evening, 2 cc's of Formula BB60 in the milk for a sound sleep

At breakfast, 2 cc's of Formula MD73 for maximum learning ability

At each meal, 1 cc of Formula Q to stay calm, reduce worry

With the above measures, plus a carefully scheduled day, it will be possible to have complete control. Through the observation monitors, it will be possible to keep strict check.

Drucy turned to me and whispered, "Those things that look like air vents."

For the first time, I realized that those so-called air vents high along the walls were actually viewers. That must have been why Drucy told me to keep low. I was so im-pressed by Drucy's courage and intelligence. I watched as she swiftly turned to the chapter that described measures to be taken in an emergency. I was afraid we didn't have much more time. My mind was swirling. No wonder the kids didn't talk much. We were drugged all the time!

Emergency Measures
If a student appears to be preparing a rebellion, or if there is any plan to escape, there will be releases into the air through the small air-cleaning jets, a mixture of RN208 in the area where the offender is. This will cause paralysis, confused thinking, and some loss of memory for a short time. All senses will be shocked by blinding lights, high-pitched sounds, and terrible odors.

I heard Drucy gasp and whisper to herself, "Wow! That's it!" And she looked up at me, her eyes wide with anger. "So that's what happened."

She closed the book, and for a few seconds, we were both too shaken to do anything. Both of us expected the same thing to happen to us right that minute. My mind was in such a whirl. I was angry at "they" for trying to control us as though we were animals, and yet, I felt a kind of sadness because we really did learn a lot of good stuff from the TV lessons.

At that moment, we were both so afraid of what we might yet meet that we tiptoed out of the meeting room into another room. This one was filled with school books and papers and supplies, shelves and shelves of supplies, all carefully labeled. I began to figure out the plan of the underground as we moved swiftly into the next room. This was a long room filled with linen and towels and all our clothes. I decided it must be underneath our dormitory.

We were both getting more and more nervous, so we hurried into the next room where we saw a whole wall of shining stainless steel drawers like file drawers. There was nothing else in the room. We saw that each stainless steel drawer had one of our names on it. Drucy went right over to the drawer with her name and tried to open it, but it was locked. We tried a few others. I saw my name. But they were all locked.

Drucy poked me and motioned that we had better hurry. When we pushed the door, we found ourselves back in the kitchen. I was confused for a second, and then I got the picture. So far, we hadn't found a way out. We went from the kitchen into a large storeroom with cleaning equipment and from there, into a room that seemed to be a film library, where tapes were stored. By this time, we were hur-rying, and when we came to the next room, we were amazed to see a big, fancy TV screen and seven leather chairs. There were cameras all around. I was scared at that moment, expecting to see some-one. Then Drucy went over to the TV and switched it on. It was a picture of us — all of us — out in the yard! It got us both so shook up, Drucy switched it off right away.

The room was darker than the others, but we both spotted, at the same time, a great big heavy door. It was the kind of big exit door found in schools. We looked at one another, and I wondered for a mo-ment if we should find our way back so we could get the other kids. Drucy gave the door a push, and it didn't open. Then I tried with her, pushing the heavy bar at the same time. Then slowly the door opened, just a tiny crack, and we could see light and sky.

"We've got to go back and get the rest of the kids," I whispered.

"Why?"

"We can't leave them."

"We'll get help first."

So we both pushed as hard as we could, and as the door opened, we heard a sharp, screaming bell, terribly loud, like the fire-drill bell. We found ourselves in bright sun-light, and when we ran up some steps, we were in what looked like a big school yard. And then we ran and ran as fast as we could while the bell kept ringing.

1st Day — Back Home

Would you believe it! When I got home, the whole family treated me as though it were just me coming home from school on any other ordinary day. I sat down at the table with my brother, Muff. He pushed over a piece of his chocolate cake and said, "Hi, Evvy. You're late today. I saved you some of my cake."

I could hardly eat that gooey thing because I felt as though it'd been so long since I'd eaten anything like that. Muff asked me what happened that I didn't like chocolate cake anymore. So I told Muff and Mom all about what had happened — where I'd been and *everything* about the Hauter experiment. I even told them about my friend Drucy.

Well, you should have seen my mom's face! And you should have heard her. Before I even finished telling my story, she got mad at me. She screamed, "So, that's what you've been doing every night when you were supposed to be sleeping. Making up another one of your crazy stories! When are you going to stop making up crazy stories! Evelyn B. Chestnut, what am I going to do with you!"

Blue Winds Dancing

by Thomas S. Whitecloud

There is a moon out tonight — moon and stars and clouds tipped with moonlight. And there is a fall wind blowing in my heart, ever since this evening, when against a fading sky I saw geese flying southward. They were going home. . . . Now I try to study, but against the pages I see them again, driving southward, going home.

Across the valley, there are heavy mountains holding up the night sky, and beyond the mountains there is home — home, and peace, and the beat of drums, and blue winds dancing over snow fields. The Indian lodge will fill with my people. I should be at home in Wisconsin. I should be at home for the winter holidays.

239

But home is beyond the mountains, and I am here at school in California. Here where fall hides in the valleys and winter never comes down from the mountains. Here where all the trees grow in rows. The palms stand stiffly by the roadsides, and in the groves, the orange trees are planted in military rows and endlessly bear fruit. Beautiful, yes; there is always beauty in order, in rows of growing things! But it is the beauty of captivity. A pine fighting for life on a windy hill is much more beautiful.

I long for the land that is my home! Home is beautiful, calm — where there is no hurry to get anywhere, no driving to keep up in a race that knows no ending and no goal. No classes where teachers talk and talk, and then stop now and then to hear their own words come back to them from the students. No constant peering into the whirlpool of one's mind. No worries about grades and honors. No long years of preparing for life. No anxiety about your place in the thing called Society.

I hear again the ring of axes in deep woods, the crunch of snow beneath my feet. I feel again the smooth velvet of birch bark. I hear the rhythm of the drums. . . .

I am tired. I want to walk again among the birches. I want to see the leaves turn in autumn and the smoke rise from the lodge houses and to feel the blue winds. I want to hear the drums; I want to hear the drums and feel the blue whispering winds.

There is a train wailing into the night. The trains go across the mountains. It would be easy to catch a freight. . . .

I find a fellow headed for Albuquerque and talk road talk with him. It is hard to ride fruit cars. It is better to wait for a cattle car going back to the Middle West and ride that, we decide. We catch the next train and walk the tops until we find a cattle car. Inside, we crouch near the forward wall, huddle, and try to sleep. I feel peaceful and content at last. I am going home. The cattle car rocks. I sleep.

Three days and several trains later, I reach Woodruff at midnight. Suddenly I am afraid, now that I am but twenty miles from home. I am afraid of what my family will say, afraid of being looked on as a stranger by my own people. I sit by a fire and think about myself and all other young Indians. We just don't seem to fit in anywhere. So many things seem to be clear now that I am away from school and do not have to worry about someone else's opinion of my ideas. It is easy to think while looking at dancing flames.

In the morning, I spend the day cleaning up and buying some presents for my family with what is left of my money. Nothing much, but a gift is a gift if you buy it with your last quarter. I wait until evening, then start up the track toward home.

Evening comes in on a north wind. Snow clouds hang over the pines, and the night comes early. Walking along the railroad bed, I feel the calm peace of snowbound forests on either side of me. I take my time. I am back in a world where time does not mean so much now. I am alone but not nearly so lonely as I was back on the campus at school. Those people who love the snow and the pines are never lonely. I walk along feeling glad because my legs are light and my feet seem to know that they are home. A deer comes out of the woods just ahead of me and stands silhouetted on the rails. The North, I feel, has welcomed me home. I watch the deer go into the woods quietly, leaving only the design of its tracks in the snow. I walk on. Now and then I pass a field, white under the night sky, with houses at the far end. Smoke comes from the chimneys of the houses, and I try to tell by the smell of the smoke what sort of wood each is burning. Some burn pine, others aspen, others tamarack. I like to watch the houses and try to imagine what might be happening in them.

Just as a light snow begins to fall, I cross the reservation boundary. Somehow it seems as though I have stepped into another world — deep woods in a snowy winter night. A faint trail leads to the village.

Laughing, I go into the woods. As I cross a frozen lake, I begin to hear the drums. Soft in the night, the drums beat. It is like the pulse beat of the world. The white line

of the lake ends at a black forest, and above the trees, the
blue winds are dancing.

I come to the first houses of the village — simple box
houses, etched black in the night. From one or two
windows, soft lamplight falls on the snow.

The village is not a sight to make you proud, yet I am
not ashamed. You can never be ashamed of your own
people when you know they have dreams as beautiful as
white snow on a tall pine.

My father and my brother and my sister are seated around the table as I walk in. Father stares at me for a moment; then I am in his arms. I give them the presents I have brought, and my throat tightens as I watch my sister carefully save bits of red string from the packages. I hide my feelings by wrestling with my brother when he strikes my shoulder as a token of affection. Father looks at me, and I know he has many questions, but he seems to know why I have come. He tells me to go on alone to the lodge, and he will follow.

I walk along the trail to the lodge, watching the northern lights forming in the heavens. Clean snow creaks beneath my feet, and a soft wind sighs through the trees, singing to me. Everything seems to say "Be happy! You are home now — you are free. You are among friends — we are your friends; we, the trees, and the snow, and the lights." I follow the trail to the lodge. My feet are light, my heart seems to sing to the music, and I hold my head high. Across white snowfields, blue winds are dancing.

Before the lodge door I stop, afraid. I wonder if my people will remember me. I stand before the door a long time. I look again at the northern lights and go in.

Inside the lodge there are many of my people. Some sit on benches around the walls. Others dance in the center of the floor around a drum. Nobody seems to notice me. It seems as though I am among a people I have never seen before. Women have children on their knees — small children who watch with serious black eyes the movements of the men dancing. The faces of the old people are serene, and their eyes are merry and bright. I look at the dark, lined faces intent on the music. I wonder if I am at all like the people here. The men dance on, lifting their feet to the rhythm of the drums, swaying slightly, looking upward. I look at their eyes and am startled at the attention to the rhythm of the music.

The dance stops. The men walk back to the walls and talk in low tones or with their hands. There is little conversation, yet everyone seems to be sharing some secret. A woman looks at a small boy wandering away, and he comes back to her.

Strange, I think, and then I remember. These people are not sharing words — they are sharing a mood. Everyone is happy. I am so used to Outside Society that it seems strange so many people can be together without someone talking. These Indians are happy because they are together, and because the night is beautiful outside, and because the music is beautiful. I try hard to forget school and Outside Society and be one of these — my people. I try to forget everything but the night and the feeling that I am with my people. We are all a part of something universal. I watch their eyes and see now that the old people are speaking to me. They nod slightly, and their eyes laugh into mine. I look around the room. All the eyes are friendly; they all laugh. No one asks why I am here. The drums begin to beat again, and I catch the invitation in the eyes of the old men. My feet begin to lift to the rhythm, and I look out beyond the walls into the night and see the lights. I am happy. It is beautiful. I am home.

i yearn

by Ricardo Sánchez

i yearn this morning
what i've yearned
since i left

   almost a year ago . . .

it is hollow
this
being away
from everyday life
in the barrios
of my homeland . . .
all those cities
like el paso, los angeles,
albuquerque,
denver, san antonio
   (off into chicano
infinitum!);

i yearn
to hear spanish
spoken in caló —
that special way
chicanos roll their
   tongues
to form
words
which dart or glide;

i yearn
for foods
that have character
and strength — the kind
that assail yet caress
you with the zest of life;

more than anything,
i yearn, my people,
for the warmth of you
greeting me with "¿qué tal,
hermano?"
and the knowing that you
   mean it
when you tell me that you love
the fact that we exist. . . .

246

CREDITS